STUD

Economics for Everybody

Applying Biblical Principles to Work, Wealth, and the World

R.C. Sproul, Jr.

Written by Thomas Purifoy, Jr.

Primary Advisor: Shawn Ritenour, Ph.D

Additional Advisors: E. Calvin Beisner, Ph.D, Paul Cleveland, Ph.D, Robert Murphy, Ph.D., and Lawrence Reed

For additional learning resources and curriculum materials go to EconomicsforEverybody.com

Contents

Welcome

Jesus taught us to pray, "Give us this day our daily bread." The provision of our daily needs matters to us, and it matters to our heavenly Father.

In this series, we are going to look at how God answers this prayer and, in His grace, gives us our daily bread. My prayer is that you will not just come away with a better understanding of how God has ordered His world, but that you will, in turn, become a more faithful steward, remembering that "the earth is the Lord's, and the fullness thereof."

In the King's Service,

R.C. Sproul, Jr.

Introduction

Welcome to the wonderful world of Economics! This study guide is intended to go with the video series of the same name, although it can be read on its own (just with less color).

The 12 Lessons in the study follow a certain sequence that may not be obvious to the casual observer. Lessons 1 to 5 introduce key economic principles; Lessons 6 and 7 explain the relationship between theology, philosophy, and economics; Lessons 9 to 12 examine the application of economics in real-life systems. Everything fits together, with each lesson generally building on the lesson before it.

This guide closely follows the material taught in the series. If you are new to economics, you may find the introduction of so many ideas makes it difficult to remember everything said. Your learning process should be helped immensely if you read the corresponding chapter in this guide after you watch the lesson.

We recommend that each person get his or her own Study Guide (or at least borrow a friend's) while going through the study.

Although there are many ways to approach the series, here are a few suggestions:

1. *Churches and small groups:* Watch one lesson per week, answer the discussion questions at the end of each chapter, and participants can read through the same chapter at home that week. In the next class, begin by reviewing what was taught the week before, answer any questions, then watch the next lesson.

2. *Middle or High School Students:* Watch one lesson per week, then read and answer the questions in the corresponding study guide chapter. To dig deeper, we recommend you purchase at least one of the textbooks recommended on the Additional Resources page. Specific chapters that go with each lesson are listed in this guide. (We also provide additional learning resources for students at www.economicsforeverybody.com.)

3. *Families and Individuals:* Pace the lessons in a way that works best for you and your family. If you like, after each lesson, you can skim through the corresponding chapter in this guide to review some of the ideas covered. Be advised that Lessons 2, 7 and 11 do have some scenes that could bother a young child. Parents may want to preview those lessons if young children are going to be watching them.

In closing, thank you for taking time to watch this series. We believe it contains information that is very important for the modern Church to hear and understand. *Soli Deo gloria.*

For Further Study

List of Additional Resources

TEXTBOOKS FROM A CHRISTIAN PERSPECTIVE

Basic Economics, 3rd Ed.—Paul Cleveland and Clarence Carson [Middle/High School and up]

Economics: Principles and Policy from a Christian Perspective, 2nd Ed.—Tom Rose [Middle/High School and up]

Foundations of Economics: A Christian View—Shawn Ritenour [Upper High School/College and up]

ECONOMIC TOPICS FROM A CHRISTIAN PERSPECTIVE

Biblical Economics: A Commonsense Guide to Our Daily Bread—R.C. Sproul, Jr

Bringing in the Sheaves: Replacing Government Welfare with Biblical Charity—George Grant

God at Work: Your Christian Vocation in All of Life—Gene Veith

Honest Money: The Biblical Blueprint for Money and Banking—Gary North*

Inherit the Earth: Biblical Blueprints for Economics—Gary North*

Money, Greed & God: Why Capitalism is the Solution and Not the Problem—Jay Richards

Prosperity and Poverty: The Compassionate Use of Resources in a World of Scarcity—E. Calvin Beisner

Unmasking the Sacred Lies—Paul Cleveland

Your Wealth in God's World—John Jefferson Davis

OTHER BOOKS

The Black Book of Communism: Crimes, Terror, Repression—Jean-Louis Panne, et al.

A Critique of Interventionism—Ludwig Von Mises*

The Commanding Heights: The Battle for the World Economy—Daniel Yergin and Joseph Stanislaw

Communism: A History—Richard Pipes

Dumbing Us Down: The Hidden Curriculum of Compulsory Schooling—John Taylor Gatto

For Good and Evil: The Impact of Taxes on the Course of Civilization—Charles Adams*

Human Action: A Treatise on Economics—Ludwig von Mises*

Index of Economic Freedom (2012)—The Heritage Foundation*

Lessons for the Young Economists—Robert Murphy*

The Mystery of Banking—Murray Rothbard*

The Politically Incorrect Guide to the Great Depression and the New Deal—Robert Murphy*

Socialism: An Economic and Sociological Analysis—Ludwig von Mises*

The Socialist Tradition: Moses to Lenin—Alexander Gray*

The State of Humanity—Julian Simon

The Welfare State: 1929–1985—Clarence Carson

The Wealth and Poverty of Nations: Why Some Are So Rich and Some So Poor—David Landes

The Wealth of Nations—Adam Smith

* Link to free downloadable version available at EconomicsForEverybody.com

1

And God Created Economics: Stewardship in God's Image

MESSAGE INTRODUCTION

The study of economics begins with God and His creation of the world. In this lesson, we will look at the implications of the creation on economics; the relationship between economics and stewardship; the cultural mandate; the reality of economics in natural law; and the connections between morality and economics.

SCRIPTURE READING

Genesis 1 & 2
Psalms 24, 104

LEARNING OBJECTIVES

1. To see that God owns everything, but that He created us to be stewards of creation for His glory.
2. To understand that God created economics to enable us to carry out the cultural mandate.
3. To recognize that there are economic laws in the world which we can learn and apply to our work as stewards.

QUOTATIONS

> *We do not, therefore, believe the teachings of economics because many people in Western Civilization have believed them, although they have. We do not believe the teachings of economics because experience verifies the truth of economics, although it does. We do not even believe the teachings of economics because all humans have rational minds which allow us to understand that humans act purposefully, although we all do have minds fitted for rational thought. We believe the truths of economics because God has created us in His image with the ability to know and perceive truth, and one of these truths communicated to us in His creation and His Word is that, like God, we act with a purpose.*
>
> —Shawn Ritenour, *Foundations of Economics*

LECTURE OUTLINE

1. Economics is a scientific discipline that applies to the choices we make in everyday life.
   A. Some people divide economics into two areas, the big picture and the little picture. They say that the principles that apply in one area do not apply in the other.
   B. But this isn't true: the economic principles that apply to individuals also apply to large, national economies. Why is this? Because all national economies are made up of individual people making individual choices. Economics always comes down to the choices of individuals.

2. Economics is the study of how God ordered the world.

   A. Sometimes it's presented in a boring, mathematical way; but this does a disservice to God and His creation. God made economics an interesting and important part of the created order. It's the way it's approached that often makes it boring.
   B. The truth is that God created economics to help man be a better steward of creation.

3. The first and most basic economic principle is this: God owns everything.
   A. God created the world *ex nihilo*, or out of nothing. Since it is His creation, it is also His possession and He can do with it as He pleases.
   B. God's creation of the world out of nothing is a demonstration of the following things:
      i. His sovereign power: God can choose to *do* whatever He wants.
      ii. His sovereign authority: God can choose to *direct* His creation to whatever end He wants.
   C. God's creation has as its purpose the manifestation of His glory. We can therefore learn specific things about God by looking at the creation.
      i. God governs the world and exercises a purposeful providence over it.
      ii. God created *natural law* to order His creation and to provide a framework within which man can live.
      iii. God does all these things not only to manifest His glory, but also to bless man.
      iv. In seeking to manifest His glory, God ultimately acts in His own self-interest—which is also in the best interest of man.

4. God created man to reflect His image. As a result, certain attributes of God are mirrored in man's attributes:
   A. Man acts with purpose.
   B. Man acts according to his preferences.
   C. Man makes choices.
   D. Man acts rationally.
   E. God designed man to do everything under His sovereign authority and for His glory.

5. God gave the first man Adam specific commands in the Garden of Eden. This is the *cultural mandate*.
   A. *And God blessed them. And God said to them, "Be fruitful and multiply and fill the earth and subdue it, and have dominion over the fish of the sea and over the birds of the heavens and over every living thing that moves on the earth." And God said, "Behold, I have given you every plant yielding seed that is on the face of all the earth, and every tree with seed in its fruit. You shall have them for food. And to every beast of the earth and to every bird of the heavens and to everything that creeps on the earth, everything that has the breath of life, I have given every green plant for food." And it was so* (Gen. 1:28–30).
   B. *The LORD God took the man and put him in the garden of Eden to work it and keep it. And the LORD God commanded the man, saying, "You may surely eat of every tree of the garden, but of the tree of the knowledge of good and evil you shall not eat, for in the day that you eat of it you shall surely die"* (Gen. 2:15–17).
   C. Since God owns all things, by putting man in charge of creation, God is making man His *steward*.

i. A steward is one who, under the authority of the owner, manages his property for the owner's benefit and good.
   ii. God gave man wisdom to be a steward, that includes discernment in making choices in light of natural limitations.
   iii. One of Adam's first stewardship activities was naming the animals.
      a. Adam had to discern the nature of each animal and make choices to put each of them into different categories.
      b. Adam showed authority over the animals by naming them, an act of control and dominion (just as parents name their own children).
      c. Adam recognized the limitations within each animal—some have two legs, some four; some swim, some fly, etc.—and named them accordingly.
   iv. In one sense, natural limitations are part of the created order. There are limitations of time and space. You can't plant two different plants in exactly the same spot. You can't mine metals in the same place you grow a garden.
      a. God gave man the ability to make wise choices in the stewardship of His creation in light of these natural limitations. In other words, some places are better for mining and some for agriculture.

6. Another important aspect of being a good steward is to recognize there are economic laws in the world.

A. Economics is man making choices as to how to best use his limited resources in order to be a good steward before God.
B. There are similarities between physical laws and economic laws, but there are also differences. Physical laws deal with inanimate objects and forces, whereas economic laws deal with living humans and their choices and actions.
C. Economics is deduced from certain premises just like geometry. In geometry, one must assume the reality of a point, a line and a plane. From those assumptions, one can draw circles, squares, or triangles, which in turn can be used to build real structures, like buildings and bridges. When an assumption is true, it works itself out in a very powerful way in the real world.
D. Economic principles are derived from the premise that humans act. Those principles provide the foundation for all the economic activity of the world. Two examples include:
    i. Gresham's Law says that if one tries to replace more valuable money with less valuable money (such as replacing gold with paper), then people will horde the good money (gold) and take it out of circulation to keep it. In effect, bad money drives out good.
    ii. The Division of Labor teaches there is an increase in productivity when work is divided up into specific callings and specializations.

7. Economics is related to morality. Because economics deals with human action and the choices we make, it is

always going to be related to ethical issues. God's commands help us to make sound economic decisions.

A. Economics is not something that can be completely understood apart from the Word of God. Like geometry, however, one does not have to know God or understand Him to employ economic principles with some effectiveness.

B. That said, unless the moral and ethical aspects of economics are recognized and ultimately acted upon, long-term economic health is impossible.

8. Why study economics?
   A. We must be obedient to the cultural mandate as children of Adam and Eve.
   B. We can grow in our prosperity if we follow the economic principles God created for our benefit.
   C. God expects us to use that prosperity for the growth of His Kingdom both locally and abroad.
   D. Ultimately, understanding economics helps us to fulfill the Great Commission.

MULTIPLE CHOICE

1. The first and most basic economic principle is: _______.
   a. Man owns private property.
   b. God owns everything.
   c. Man is to be God's steward.
   d. Economics is a scientific discipline.

2. Economics is primarily a study of man's _______.
   a. Reason
   b. Nature
   c. Choices
   d. Money

3. A steward is one who, under the authority of the owner, manages his property for _______.
   a. personal gain
   b. the welfare of others
   c. the best use of his family
   d. the owner's benefit and good

4. Because economics deals with _______, it is always going to be related to ethical issues.
   a. human action
   b. monetary function
   c. fiscal management
   d. resource allocation

5. Why study economics?
   a. We must be obedient to the cultural mandate as children of Adam and Eve.
   b. We can grow in our prosperity if we follow the economic principles God created for our benefit.
   c. God expects us to use that prosperity for the growth of His Kingdom both locally and abroad.
   d. All of the above.

SHORT ANSWER

1. Explain the relationship between stewardship and economics.

2. Name some ways that the cultural mandate is related to economics in your own life.

3. Why do you think economics is often divorced from morality in the modern world?

4. How might economics enable us to fulfill the Great Commission beyond just providing missionaries with financial support?

DISCUSSION

1. Almost everyone today agrees that economics is important. But many will say they are confused by it. Why do you think that is? If understanding economics is important to men and women being faithful stewards, what might be the reasons it is not widely taught either in society or the church?
2. What are some of the ways that economics is related to morality?
3. If economics is 'man making choices as to how to best use his limited resources in order to be a good steward before God,' what are some specific ways you act economically in your particular calling?

FOR FURTHER STUDY

Foundations of Economics—Ritenour—Introduction, Chapter 1
Basic Economics, 3rd Ed.—Carson & Cleveland—Chapters 1–2
Prosperity and Poverty—Beisner—Introduction

Multiple choice answers: 1.b 2.c 3.d 4.a 5.d

2

The Economic Problem of Sin: Law, Liberty and Government

MESSAGE INTRODUCTION

Sin is one of the primary issues that affects economics. In this lesson, we will look at the impact of the fall on economics; the way sin affects our relationships to the creation and to other men and women; the economic results of the Law and the Ten Commandments; the importance of liberty; and the role of civil government.

SCRIPTURE READING

Genesis 3–9

Exodus 20

Romans 13

LEARNING OBJECTIVES

1. To understand the impact of sin on economics.
2. To see the importance of the Law to economic growth.
3. To recognize the role of civil government in any economic system.

QUOTATIONS

God promises prosperity and blessing to societies that abide by His Law. But He warns of misery and judgment on those who reject it. The prosperity and blessing, on the one hand, and the misery and judgment, on the other, are not solely caused by God's response to our actions. They are also the natural, cause-and-effect results of behavior consistent or inconsistent with the moral and physical laws God has woven into the fabric of creation. The Biblical worldview, by recognizing these laws and teaching people to operate consistently with them, underlies the prosperity of the West.

—E. Calvin Beisner, *Prosperity and Poverty*

LECTURE OUTLINE

1. The impact of the Fall of Adam and Eve extended to all of creation.
   A. Before the Fall, it's difficult to imagine how rich and fertile the original garden must have been.
   B. As a result of Adam's sin, however, God told Adam: *"Cursed is the ground because of you; in pain you shall eat of it all the days of your life; thorns and thistles it shall bring forth for you; and you shall eat the plants of the field. By the sweat of your face you shall eat bread, till you return to the ground..."* (Gen. 3:17–19).
   C. God's curse of the ground means there is now *scarcity* beyond the natural limitations of space and time. Scarcity is the problem of a cursed ground that will not naturally provide for man's needs. Scarcity greatly worsens the challenge of natural limitations.

D. As a result of the curse and the problem of scarcity, the basic question of man's life is now 'How will I survive from day to day?'

2. Scarcity combined with sin and ignorance consistently leads to poverty.
   A. Although the nations of the West have been prosperous for centuries, the majority of the world's population has been poor through most of world history. It remains that way for billions of people today.
   B. No system of economics is going to eradicate poverty. History shows us, however, that some economic systems tend toward increasing poverty while other systems tend toward lessening poverty.
   C. Since we, as Christians, are interested in reducing poverty, we should also be interested in the economic system that works best to marginalize and reduce poverty as well as to help us be better stewards of God's creation.
   D. Stewardship is man governing and using the created order for God's purposes and for God's glory.

3. The Fall has greatly affected who we are as men and women made in the image of God. This includes the economic work God desires us to do.
   A. We do not think in a rational way with consistency.
   B. We ignore our calling as stewards under God's authority.
   C. We work for our own purposes instead of God's purposes.
   D. We find ways to steal, to lie, and to exploit other men, especially through various forms of slavery.

E. A comparison of the line of Cain with the line of Seth in the first chapters of Genesis shows the radical departure within Cain's line from what God intended.
   i. Lamech, of the line of Cain, said to his wives: *"Adah and Zillah, hear my voice; you wives of Lamech, listen to what I say: I have killed a man for wounding me, a young man for striking me. If Cain's revenge is sevenfold, then Lamech's is seventy-sevenfold"* (Gen. 4:23–24).
   ii. But in the line of Seth: *Enoch walked with God after he fathered Methuselah 300 years and had other sons and daughters. Thus all the days of Enoch were 365 years. Enoch walked with God, and he was not, for God took him* (Gen. 5:22–24).
F. The cultural mandate and God's call to stewardship remain, but our sinful natures prevent us from being able to fulfill them without God's grace.

4. Whenever we are overcome by sin, God intervenes in our lives to save us from ourselves.
   A. He gives us His law to provide boundaries within which we can find prosperity. Moses said, *"And if you faithfully obey the voice of the LORD your God, being careful to do all his commandments that I command you today, the LORD your God will set you high above all the nations of the earth. And all these blessings shall come upon you and overtake you, if you obey the voice of the LORD your God"* (Deut. 28:1–2).
   B. He demonstrates His grace to us by redeeming us from judgment and blessing us in our obedience.
   C. The story of Noah is a picture of God's call to stewardship and blessing.

i. Noah was given a specific economic task to build an ark using land, labor and capital. Noah's obedience was an example of godly stewardship.
ii. God saved Noah and blessed his obedience, then repeated to Noah the cultural mandate: *And God blessed Noah and his sons and said to them, "Be fruitful and multiply and fill the earth"* (Gen. 9:1).
iii. God also gave Noah specific commands that helped him and his family live on the land. God did this to a much greater degree when He gave Moses His Laws on Mt. Sinai.

5. Most people don't think about economics when they think about the Ten Commandments, but they provide the cultural and legal framework necessary for a people to create a community in which they can be stewards under God.
   A. Although the Ten Commandments have a personal aspect to them, they also have a corporate, societal aspect that has great bearing on our economic lives.
   B. The Ten Commandments (Exodus 20) are divided into two tables, one dealing with our relationship to God and the other with our relationship to man. Both sets of relationships are important to economics.
      i. *You shall have no other gods before me.*—The first commandment tells us that all aspects of our lives must be lived in submission to God as faithful stewards.
      ii. *You shall not make for yourself a carved image, or any likeness of anything that is in heaven above, or that is in the earth beneath, or that is*

in the water under the earth. You shall not bow down to them or serve them...—The second commandment tells us that we must not make idols of anybody in our community or of anything that we can create, whether it be products, tools, or services.

iii. *You shall not take the name of the LORD your God in vain...*—The third commandment tells us not to exploit the name of God as if it were some magic talisman to bring us power, wealth and economic success.

iv. *Remember the Sabbath day, to keep it holy. Six days you shall labor, and do all your work, but the seventh day is a Sabbath to the LORD your God.*—The fourth commandment not only commands us to rest, but also commands us to work. We see that the Biblical ratio of work to rest means that 6 days out of a week should be spent working as stewards in the callings God has given us, both inside and outside the home.

v. *Honor your father and your mother, that your days may be long in the land that the LORD your God is giving you.*—The fifth commandment establishes a framework of authority and submission that starts with the family. Recognizing the authority structures that pervade society, then honoring them, is a pathway to blessing and prosperity.

vi. *You shall not murder.*—The sixth commandment establishes the protection of life as the foundation of any healthy society. History shows that societies that do not protect life quickly succumb to economic catastrophe: it is impossible to work and trade for long in an environment of death.

vii. *You shall not commit adultery.*—The seventh commandment shows us the importance of protecting marriage and families through the laws of a society. Marriages of one man and one woman producing healthy families are the building blocks of any civilization: families are the self-perpetuating method God uses to grow up godly boys and girls to work as faithful stewards with their own families. A society that disregards the importance of marriage and family erodes the walls that support the entire economy.

viii. *You shall not steal.*—The eighth commandment establishes the economic principle of private property; that is, individuals have the right to own things and to choose to do what they want with them. Stealing is taking someone's private property without his permission. A healthy economic system prohibits stealing at all levels (including stealing by the government).

ix. *You shall not bear false witness against your neighbor.*—The ninth commandment sets up the groundwork for statements of fact, agreements, and contracts. Telling the truth is basic for economic life: one must be able to depend on the integrity of other people to engage in effective long-term trade and business relationships.

x. *You shall not covet your neighbor's house; you shall not covet your neighbor's wife, or his male servant, or his female servant, or his ox, or his donkey, or anything that is your neighbor's.*—The tenth commandment is perhaps surprising in its economic context, but it makes perfect sense in light of man's insatiable greed. Covetousness is often the root of our exploitation of others, when we're unhappy with the way God has blessed us in comparison to them. An economy made up of people who strive not to covet would be a prosperous economy indeed.

6. God has not only given us His Law, but He has given us the civil government as a means of enforcing laws in society.
   a. God established the authority of civil government in the world when He spoke to Noah after leaving the ark: "*And for your lifeblood I will require a reckoning: from every beast I will require it and from man. From his fellow man I will require a reckoning for the life of man. Whoever sheds the blood of man, by man shall his blood be shed, for God made man in his own image*" (Gen. 9:5–6).
   b. Civil government is an agency of force. It 'wields the sword' of governmental coercion, and therefore has the ability to take the lives of those under its rule. As Genesis 9 points out, there are some biblically-justified instances of capital punishment.
   c. Yet it is not only in the Old Testament, but also in the New, that the sphere of civil government is affirmed. Paul says in his letter to the Romans: "*Let every person be subject to the governing authorities. For there is no authority except from God, and those that exist have been instituted by God. Therefore whoever resists the authorities resists what God has appointed, and those*

who resist will incur judgment. For rulers are not a terror to good conduct, but to bad. Would you have no fear of the one who is in authority? Then do what is good, and you will receive his approval, for he is God's servant for your good. But if you do wrong, be afraid, for he does not bear the sword in vain. For he is the servant of God, an avenger who carries out God's wrath on the wrongdoer. Therefore one must be in subjection, not only to avoid God's wrath but also for the sake of conscience. For because of this you also pay taxes, for the authorities are ministers of God, attending to this very thing. Pay to all what is owed to them: taxes to whom taxes are owed, revenue to whom revenue is owed, respect to whom respect is owed, honor to whom honor is owed" (Rom. 13:1–7).

D. According to these passages, the primary role of civil government is to set down the rule of law and to punish evildoers. This view of government is an extremely limited view compared to that of modern governments that redistribute wealth, take care of the poor, and engage in countless economic endeavors.

E. Instead, the biblical role of government establishes a fence and boundary within which a people can live and grow economically as stewards of God's creation. This "rule of law" includes protection of life, property, marriage and family, defense against invaders, and upholds the integrity of agreements and contracts.

F. Yet the power of the sword provides a dangerous temptation to those inside and outside the government. Historically, people have vied with one another for control of that sword to oppress others while they benefited themselves. Liberty and tyranny are the two opposite extremes that struggle with each other for control of the government. The former seeks to limit government to its natural province, while the latter seeks to expand it to do its will.

7. There is a clear connection between obedience to God's commands and national economic prosperity.
   A. History demonstrates that those nations that were most influenced by the Protestant Reformation (Germany, Great Britain, Switzerland, the United States, the Netherlands, Scandinavia, and others) have historically enjoyed the greatest prosperity in the world. Other European and European-influenced nations that have followed a Christian view of the world stand close beside them.
   B. Why is this? It is because our corporate understanding of God influences how we understand what man is. In other words, our theology ultimately influences our economics. We can see it in this sequence:
      i. The study of God (theology)
      ii. Leads to believing certain things about man (anthropology)
      iii. Which in turn informs a political philosophy
      iv. And political system,
      v. Which ultimately provides a foundation for an economic philosophy
      vi. And economic system.
   C. As we pursue this study, we will see that what we believe about God ultimately determines whether we will enjoy prosperity and liberty or whether we will live in poverty and tyranny.

MULTIPLE CHOICE

1. _______ is the problem of a cursed ground that will not naturally provide for man's needs.
   a. Death
   b. Food
   c. Scarcity
   d. Dust
2. The cultural mandate and God's call to stewardship remain, but _______ prevent us from being able to fulfill them without God's grace.
   a. our sinful natures
   b. natural laws
   c. our tendencies to exploit others
   d. our premature deaths
3. The Ten Commandments provide the _______ necessary for a people to create a community in which they can be stewards under God.
   a. personal ethical standards
   b. cultural and legal framework
   c. elementary rules
   d. economic laws
4. Civil government is an agency of _______.
   a. taxation
   b. welfare
   c. provision
   d. force
5. Our _______ ultimately influences our economics.
   a. ontology
   b. teleology
   c. theology
   d. eschatology

SHORT ANSWER

1. Explain why some economic systems tend toward increasing poverty while other systems tend toward decreasing it.

2. Why is the law so important for economics? For personal liberty?

3. What are some economic roles the civil government has taken on in the modern world? What does the Bible say (or not say) about those roles?

DISCUSSION

1. Some people have referred to the 'grace of law.' How is law a grace in terms of our economic lives?
2. How does sin exacerbate a nation's economic problems, especially in those countries that reject God?
3. What are some specific ways the Ten Commandments are necessary for a healthy economic life?

FOR FURTHER STUDY

Basic Economics, 3rd Ed.—Carson & Cleveland—Chapters 3–4
Prosperity and Poverty—Beisner—Chapters 11, 14
Biblical Economics—Sproul—Chapter 9

Multiple choice answers: 1.c 2.a. 3.b 4.d 5.c

3

The Path from Work to Wealth: Production, Property and Tools

MESSAGE INTRODUCTION

There are some key economic principles that lead to prosperity. In this lesson, we'll look at positive and negative views of wealth; at the importance of work; at the means of production; at private property; at savings; at the division of labor; and at mass production.

SCRIPTURE READING

Exodus 35

1 Kings 5–6

LEARNING OBJECTIVES

1. To understand some of the economic principles that lead to prosperity.
2. To see that everything productive relies on individual work.
3. To recognize the importance of trade and cooperation as the building blocks of economic growth.

QUOTATIONS

"Among civilized and thriving nations...though a great number of people do not labor at all, many of whom

consume the produce of ten times, frequently of a hundred times more labor than the greater part of those who work; yet the produce of the whole labor of the society is so great, that all are often abundantly supplied, and a workman, even of the lowest and poorest order, if he is frugal and industrious, may enjoy a greater share of the necessities and conveniences of life than it is possible for any savage to acquire."

—Adam Smith, *The Wealth of Nations*

LECTURE OUTLINE

1. Wealth can be defined as the ability to acquire the things that we want and need.
   A. Conversely, poverty could be defined as not being able to acquire the things that we need.
   B. Once we have everything we need, all that is left is acquiring the things that we want.
   C. The Bible gives warnings against having too great a desire for things that we may want but do not need: *And [Jesus] said to them, "Take care, and be on your guard against all covetousness, for one's life does not consist in the abundance of his possessions"* (Luke 12:15).
   D. But this is a warning against covetousness and greed; it's not a statement that wealth is a bad thing in itself. In fact, the Bible teaches that *Everyone also to whom God has given wealth and possessions and power to enjoy them, and to accept his lot and rejoice in his toil—this is the gift of God* (Ecc. 5:19). After all, some of the most blessed men in the Bible were wealthy: think of Noah, Abraham, Isaac, Jacob, David, Solomon and many more.

E. It's also not wrong to want to live in a wealthy nation that is prosperous, in which there are few truly poor people, and in which many men and women can freely serve God with all their resources.

F. Adam Smith, the great Scottish economist, entitled his most famous work *An Inquiry into the Causes and Nature of the Wealth of Nations*. We know it today simply as *The Wealth of Nations*, but we can see from its title what he was really interested in: 'why are some nations rich and other nations poor?' It is still an important question today.

2. The truth is that there are some basic economic principles that consistently create wealth. The key to understanding why some nations (or individuals) are rich and others poor is recognizing these basic principles that consistently lead to wealth.

3. Principle #1 : God made us for work.

   A. Just as God accomplished His creation with work, so must all our creative activities be accomplished with work. *And on the seventh day God finished his work that he had done, and he rested on the seventh day from all his work that he had done* (Gen. 2:2).

   B. God has created each man and woman with unique gifts, abilities, skills and, in His providence, has placed us in different times and places. All of these things harmonize together to establish our *vocation* or calling.

   C. We see from God's first command to Adam that He intended him to work on the creation. Furthermore, it shows us that work is good in itself. Although God may have cursed the ground so that work is now much more difficult, it does not mean that work itself is cursed. Rather, work is what God calls every man and woman to do as stewards of His creation.

4. Principle #2 : Work is productive activity.
   A. In our modern world, one of the problems we face is that the work we do is not always matched to our vocational skills. As a result, it is easy for some people to see work as a drudgery and almost a waste of time.
   B. From the beginning, however, God intended work to be productive activity. Work is taking one part of God's creation and reshaping it into something more useful. Think about a farmer growing crops, a craftsman creating a table, or a doctor curing a patient. Each is creating something new through his productive work. There are countless ways in which we can produce things in our society. They are always the result of work.

5. Principle #3 : Man owns what he produces.
   A. There is a basic logic to man owning the fruit of his labor. It goes all the way back to Cain and Abel: *Now Abel was a keeper of sheep, and Cain a worker of the ground. In the course of time Cain brought to the LORD an offering of the fruit of the ground, and Abel also brought of the firstborn of his flock...* (Gen. 4:2–4). Neither could offer to God what he did not already own and control.
   B. The things that individual men and women own are generally known as *private property*. This principle of private property lies at the root of all wealth

production. Although there are some economic philosophies that deny private property and its benefits, from Genesis to Revelation God consistently affirms the right to individuals in their stewardship and production of wealth.

C. When we produce things, we're producing what are known as *economic goods*, such as apples or hammers or mobile phones. The production of economic goods always comes through the intermingling of *three factors of production*: *land, labor and capital goods.*
   i. Land is not just a plot of ground, but rather the whole of the created order: trees, metals, mountains, water, animals, and so forth. It refers to all those things created by God for our use.
   ii. Labor refers to the work that we do either on the land itself or on the capital we have created through labor with the land. Labor includes all the energy we expend doing productive activity on the earth.
   iii. Capital goods refers to those things that are used to create other things. Machines in a factory, tractors on a farm, and paints in an artist's studio are also considered capital. The accumulation of capital is one of the marks of wealth for a society. Why? Because it means that a society is able to be more and more effective in its work.

D. Economic goods also include economic services that may not include the transfer of an object, but is the transfer of work. For instance, the work of a doctor, or an accountant, or a consultant (or countless other services) are not tangible in the same way as an apple, but they are equally valuable types of productive activity.

6. Principle #4 : We need to be able to exchange goods and services with one another.
   A. God never intended man to be alone. When we see that men and women have unique vocations and therefore create different kinds of goods and services, then it makes sense to see how a community of people working together and exchanging with one another is at the heart of a functioning, healthy civilization.
   B. When people freely exchange what they have for something they desire more, they are involved in an exchange that benefits *both* of them. Each exchange is just a small step in the pathway toward increasing wealth. After all, one man gives away what he wants less to gain what he wants more—otherwise he wouldn't give away what he has.
   C. We refer to this exchange as *trade*, and it occurs at all sorts of levels in all sorts of places, literally billions of times a day around the world. From the simple trade of someone giving their money in exchange for someone else's labor to cut their lawn, to the complex trade that happens in a stock exchange, trade is the way an economy grows and prospers.
   D. What do people do with some of the things they receive in trades or create by production? (That is, those things that aren't used to produce other things.) They are an important part of any economic system.

People have to eat and wear clothes and use phones and drive cars and so forth. But once an economic good is consumed, it is gone—there is nothing else it can be used for. So how do we ensure that we continually have enough for the future?

7. Principle #5 : We have to save our surplus in order to accumulate capital to be used in more complex production.
   A. This principle follows from the earlier principles we stated. If work is productive activity that uses land, labor and capital to create goods to trade with other people, then the only way to produce more complex goods is to gather together and save enough capital to create them.
   B. Just think about the amount of capital that goes into making something as simple as a pencil:
      i. The wood has to be cut down by chainsaws, delivered to mills by trucks, cut by band saws, planed by machines, stacked onto other trucks...
      ii. The graphite has to be mined or created by machines and chemicals plus materials, then shaped by other machines, put onto trucks...
      iii. The paint has to come from natural and artificial pigments, added to chemicals made by large chemical manufacturing plants using other more basic chemicals, then put in metal drums and shipped on trucks...
      iv. The metal has to be mined from the ground as ore by drills and other earth-moving equipment, melted in furnaces, purified in factories, cooled, put on trucks...

v. The eraser comes from rubber trees and is collected, processed by factories, colored, and shipped on ships across the sea...
vi. Then, when all these things come together in one factory, there are more machines to assemble, paint, box, and then—guess what –put on more trucks and deliver to a store near you.
vii. And what about the capital that goes into making a truck? You can only imagine how complex and how many endless pieces go into *that* process.

C. Here's an important thing to understand: it is the saving and accumulation of capital that is the *primary* reason why the Western nations are so materially advanced beyond other nations in the world. Our forefathers in the eighteenth, nineteenth and early twentieth centuries understood basic economics and so saved capital to create more complex things, which they in turn accumulated together to create even more complex things, and so on and so forth to create a civilization more massively wealthy and technologically advanced than any other civilization before it. But it is founded on understanding how best to use capital.
D. That said, if this same civilization begins to consume more than it saves, then it will slowly grow poorer as it loses more and more capital necessary for true economic development and growth.

8. Principle #6: If men work together and cooperate, they can combine their land, labor, and capital to multiply their abilities to produce even greater and more complex things. Furthermore they can specialize in what they're best at producing. This is called the *division of labor.*

A. Division of labor was the first concept Adam Smith wrote about in *The Wealth of Nations*. He looked at a small nail factory and saw how the division of different parts of the work into specific jobs enabled people to pool their abilities to create far more nails together than they ever could separately.

B. Division of labor is related in many ways to the idea of vocation when it is looked at on a larger scale. Remember our pencil analogy: some companies provided the metal, some the wood, some the paint, and so forth. This also applies to software development, building cars, and countless other things produced in the world today.

   i. Here is a picture of the complex division of labor that went into building the tabernacle: *Let every skillful craftsman among you come and make all that the LORD has commanded: the tabernacle, its tent and its covering, its hooks and its frames, its bars, its pillars, and its bases; the ark with its poles, the mercy seat, and the veil of the screen; the table with its poles and all its utensils, and the bread of the Presence; the lampstand also for the light, with its utensils and its lamps, and the oil for the light; and the altar of incense, with its poles, and the anointing oil and the fragrant incense, and the screen for the door, at the door of the tabernacle; the altar of burnt offering, with its grating of bronze, its poles, and all its utensils, the basin and its stand; the hangings of the court, its pillars and its bases, and the screen for the gate of the court; the pegs of the tabernacle and the pegs of the court, and their cords; the finely worked garments for ministering in the Holy Place, the holy garments for Aaron the priest, and the garments of his sons, for their service as priests* (Ex. 35:10–19).

C. Why is division of labor so important? It relies upon cooperation and the combination of various skills to accomplish its goals. It is a principle based on the point that God created communities of people to work together in harmony. We are meant to utilize the skills and work of each other since we are all created differently.

D. Of course, division of labor applies to people working together in a variety of settings. The social division of labor enables people to work in all the different lines of production that make up the modern world. It continues to be used in factories around the world, and although sometimes these jobs are looked down upon by some in the modern West, it is important to remember that many people around the world take them willingly compared to other things they could be doing—as did many of our forefathers hundreds of years ago.

E. One of the great benefits of division of labor is the *saving of time*. When people work together, they can accomplish much more in less time than they ever could working independently. This saved time can then be used for any number of things, whether it be leisure activities or time to research new ways to produce and work more efficiently: such as the creation of new tools and technologies.

9. Principle #7 : Capital in the form of tools enables us to create things of greater complexity that we might otherwise not have been able to create.
   A. What are *tools*? They can be as simple as a pair of knitting needles, to a computer, to a truck, to a hydroelectric dam. All of these things are tools because they are used to increase our productivity.
   B. Tools are the building blocks of every civilization. The Egyptian empire had its tools, as did the Roman, as did the Carolingian, and so forth. But what we see in the modern world is that the more complex the tools are, the more productive the civilization can be.
   C. The ongoing specialization and complication of successive generations of tools have resulted in such spectacular machines as microcomputers, satellites and jets, as well as countless other things that fill our modern world.
   D. Of course, today almost everything that we use and consume is created by a tool or series of tools. It is this grand proliferation of tools and capital that enables goods to be mass produced in factories.

10. Principle #8 : When goods are mass produced, the increased quantity drives prices down, which in turn enables them to be purchased by still more people.
    A. Although we will talk about supply, demand and prices in another lesson, recognize for now that an increased supply of goods normally leads to a decrease in price for those goods.
    B. Mass production is what enables us to have affordable homes, clothes, computers, food, and so forth. Mass

production is everywhere in the modern world, and it is a good thing in many ways.

C. It was another observation of Adam Smith's that what is important is not how much money you have, but what that money will buy you. This is known as *purchasing power*.
D. When goods are mass-produced and prices drop, it means that the purchasing power of individual people increases, including those with less money.
E. Mass production is one of the great economic principles that keeps prices lower compared to what they would be if goods were produced individually. Furthermore, mass production enables people to specialize more and more in certain areas knowing that they can freely trade with one another through an ever-expanding selection of goods and services.

11. All these principles can be tied together in a chain: Work and productive activity + private property + free exchange + savings + division of labor + tools + mass production + lower prices = an ever-widening spiral of prosperity for a nation.
    A. If wealth is the ability to acquire the things that we want and need, then when prices drop on an ever-widening supply of goods and services, all people in a society benefit.
    B. In fact, it's not primarily the wealthy that benefit, but those at the bottom of the economic ladder who are themselves able to enjoy greater and greater prosperity. A simple comparison with the average poor person in the West with the average poor person

in Asia reveals the extreme differences in material wealth for even the poorest members of our society. This is not to make light of those at the bottom of the economic chain, but to prove that even poverty is relative between nations that are generally wealthy and generally poor. Wealth-building is not a blessing of the haves at the expense of the have-nots, but a general rising of all boats together.

12. It's not a coincidence that those nations at the forefront of implementing these economic principles in their societies were those nations that were grounded in the thinking of the Protestant Reformation:
    A. England led the economic revolution in the eighteenth century, with countries like Germany, Switzerland, Scandinavia and the United States not far behind.
    B. The other nations of Europe that held to a different, but still Christian worldview, developed in the same direction and today boast the same economic successes when compared with other parts of the world.
    C. These principles can only work together in the context of law, peace and protection that we saw in our previous lesson. It is true that men remain sinners, and so governmental protections are necessary for these principles to be followed by an entire society. The chain of events will quickly break down without integrity in contracts, protection of life and property, and the other laws necessary for a healthy and functioning society.
    D. Finally, the wealth that comes from this economic prosperity should be used for:

i. The expansion of God's Kingdom. Not only are we building up the local church and its ministries, we are regularly sending out missionaries around the world and financing them with the surplus from our work.
ii. The creation of art. The spare time we have is often used for writing novels, painting artwork, and other creative activities.
iii. The betterment of individuals in need. Charitable giving is increased when there are more surpluses due to free exchange and more efficient, increased production. This is a great blessing from God.

MULTIPLE CHOICE

1. God made us for ________.
   a. economics
   b. property
   c. work
   d. money
2. The principle of ________ lies at the root of all wealth production.
   a. private property
   b. wealth allocation
   c. resource management
   d. work organization
3. The means of production are ________.
   a. money, markets and capital
   b. land, exports and labor
   c. trade, labor and wealth
   d. land, labor and capital

4. _______ relies upon cooperation and the combination of various skills to accomplish its goals.
   a. Trade unionism
   b. Division of labor
   c. Means of production
   d. Work

5. What is important is not how much money you have, but what that money will buy you. This is known as _______.
   a. capital gains
   b. wealth application
   c. purchasing power
   d. monetary effectiveness

SHORT ANSWER

1. Explain why free trade is the engine for economic growth in a society. How does it create wealth?

2. What is the relationship between tools, capital accumulation, and the wealth of the modern world? How does that relate to the cultural mandate?

3. Explain how the principles listed in this lesson work together to overcome scarcity and to create prosperity for a nation.

DISCUSSION

1. Talk through the links in the chain from work to wealth. Do you understand how they all link together and why this is so powerful? What happens if specific links are missing?
2. Consider your own vocation: are you designed to be doing what you're doing, or are you frustrated in your job? If the latter, what steps can you take to better fulfill the way God made you? Success comes when we're doing what we're made to do.
3. Look at some common items around you and talk through all the steps and materials necessary to create them.
4. If American Christians have been blessed with great prosperity, what does God expect them to do with it? Do you think you are spending more time trying to build up your bank account for your own gratification, or trying to use the resources God has given you to build up His Kingdom?

FOR FURTHER STUDY

Basic Economics, 3rd Ed.—Carson & Cleveland—Chapters 5–7, 11
Foundations of Economics—Ritenour—Chapter 4
Prosperity and Poverty—Beisner—Chapters 2, 6–7
Biblical Economics—Sproul—Chapter 4

Multiple choice answers: 1.c 2.a 3.d 4.b 5.c

4

The Route from Scarcity to Plenty: Money, Markets and Trade

MESSAGE INTRODUCTION

God has put certain economic relationships in place that enable us to overcome the natural scarcity in the world. In this lesson, we'll look at economic value; the nature of free markets and trade; the purpose of money; the role of prices; the laws of supply and demand; and the law of marginal utility.

SCRIPTURE READING

Genesis 41

2 Kings 6:24–7:20

LEARNING OBJECTIVES

1. To understand God's economic design for free markets and trade.
2. To see how money and prices work together to reflect value.
3. To recognize the way the laws of supply, demand and marginal utility enable markets to provide for a society.

QUOTATIONS

> *When unions get higher wages for their members by restricting entry into an occupation, those higher wages are at the expense of other workers who find their opportunities reduced. When government pays its employees higher wages, those higher wages are at the expense of the taxpayer. But when workers get higher wages and better working conditions through the free market, when they get raises by firms competing with one another for the best workers, by workers competing with one another for the best jobs, those higher wages are at nobody's expense. They can only come from higher productivity, greater capital investment, more widely diffused skills. The whole pie is bigger—there's more for the worker, but there's also more for the employer, the investor, the consumer, and even the tax collector. That's the way the free market system distributes the fruits of economic progress among all people. That's the secret of the enormous improvements in the conditions of the working person over the past two centuries.*
>
> —Milton Friedman

LECTURE OUTLINE

1. What do famines teach us about scarcity and plenty?
   A. History attests to the prevalence of famines. They are common around the world and have been throughout history.
   B. During a famine, great scarcity drives prices up even on less desirable goods. This is what we see during a siege of Jerusalem recorded in 2 Kings 6 & 7. The head of a donkey is worth 80 shekels. Yet once the siege is lifted and food is suddenly available, prices fall again

to normal levels and a donkey's head is worthless. This story highlights the extreme contrast between scarcity and plenty.

C. Although famines have been common throughout history, there has never been a true famine in the United States. Why is that? It's because there are economic principles that enable a society to move beyond scarcity and toward plenty.

D. We have already talked about some of those principles: law and liberty provide a context for work, production and trade. This productive process enables us to create more of the things we need and want.

E. But how do we know what to produce? And how much to produce of it? Who tells us when to produce it, and where to sell it? These are all questions of economic *value*.

2. What is value? Value is the way we judge the worth of things. Everyone on the planet is making all sorts of judgments about all sorts of things every day, and those judgments go back to each person's unique sense of economic value.

   A. We're not talking about moral values, but economic value. Moral values are absolute and objective in terms of right and wrong: do not murder, do not steal, do not lie, and so forth.

   B. Economic value, however, is changeable and subjective. Some people prefer chocolate to vanilla ice cream and therefore value one more than the other; the worth they place on each is based on their unique makeup and circumstances. But, if they are offered vanilla ice cream vs. mud-flavored ice cream, their sense of worth would quickly shift.

C. This situation highlights the complex nature of economic value: it is an internal scale within each person that constantly changes based on a variety of things. Someone may want a raincoat, someone else prefers an umbrella, and someone may want both. In a free economy, individuals bring their values to the marketplace and seek to satisfy them through exchanges.
D. This explains why there are so many different things out there: there are countless different consumers all with unique values that are being satisfied by different producers offering different goods and services.
E. Yet, it gets more complex because there are *limitations* to the things available at any one time. Economists refer to these limitations as scarcity. There may only be so many raincoats available in a particular style in one season and they sell out; or there could be a hurricane and the value of raincoats goes up suddenly, and all the raincoats available are purchased. Value concerning goods and services shifts very quickly, and limitations are part of that process.
F. Finally, value doesn't apply only to the goods and services we buy, but it also applies to the work we do, how we spend our leisure time, and many more of our daily decisions. All of these decisions based on various desires have to be prioritized because of limitations.

3. What happens when desires come together and a trade is made? Markets are created.
   A. When your desire for one thing comes together with your neighbor's desire for that same thing as well as lots of other people's matching desires (such as

a desire for chocolate ice cream), we call all these consumers together that are able to buy a *demand*. Demand just describes the similar values of lots of people who desire and are able to make an exchange. For instance, there is a demand for chocolate ice cream. Or for apple juice, or for cell phones, or for Swedish massages, or for countless other things.

B. When people have the desire and ability to make a purchase, they look for people who actually produce chocolate ice cream or apple juice or cell phones. On the opposite side, these producers together create what we call a *supply*.

C. When people with a desire and the ability to consume (a demand) meet up with those who have a product and the ability to sell (a supply), then an exchange will potentially be made. What this is called is a *market*.

D. Markets are just an interchange between people with different desires. You come to the market and trade what you have that you value less (money) for what someone else has that you value more (chocolate ice cream). The seller, on the other hand, values the chocolate ice cream less than he values your money. So a trade occurs that everyone is happy with.

E. Trade within markets happens every day in all sorts of ways: in grocery stores, gas stations, stock exchanges, real estate brokerages, farmers markets, etc, etc.

F. When no one is being coerced by anyone else in their trade, then the market is considered a *free market*. This means that people enter into agreements voluntarily.

4. Markets were designed by God for men and women to grow in wealth and prosperity by trading with one another.
    A. Markets enable people to freely come and engage in trade to get what they want or need through cooperation with one another.
    B. God designed the market to give us the opportunity to exercise our free choices to minister to one another as well as to pursue our own self-interests.
    C. Markets are how we cooperate in pursuit of our self-interest so that everybody benefits. After all, when we trade voluntarily there's no such thing as an even trade, or a trade where someone gains and someone loses. Rather, when two people make a trade that they freely agree upon, they both gain. That is, they each give up what they value less to get what they value more—and walk away feeling they got what they wanted.
    D. Markets are God's solution to limitation and scarcity. When we take into consideration our wants and needs as well as the limitations of the natural order, this is how we determine how we're going to get the things we value most and give up the things we value least.
    E. If you look back in history, this is how things have always worked: since the beginning, people have formed markets to freely exchange with one another in order to fulfill their needs and wants.

5. Experience shows us that trade based on barter is rather limited. So almost all societies have developed a common medium of exchange known as *money*.

A. Money enables us to do trades in a far more complex way with a far wider reach to far more people. Why is that?
B. Money serves as a *unit of account*. This means that money prices are objective amounts that manifest people's subjective values. They help people to compare value in a way that crosses from person to person and from sphere to sphere. For instance, if you're willing to pay $5 for a basket of apples but $50 for a tire, then it shows that you value a tire a lot more than you value a basket of apples. Or if you trade $5 for a book, and the bookstore owner trades that $5 for a gallon of milk, and the grocery store owner trades the same $5 for a box of lightbulbs, then we can generally know that all those things are valued about the same in terms of money.
C. This reveals to us that money also serves as a *store of value*. In our example, as money moved from person to person, it kept its value even though new people had the same $5 at different times and places. For instance, if you want to sell something now, then buy something later, money should hold its value so you can trade at different times with the same units and same value.
D. If money prices are objective amounts that manifest people's subjective values, then how do we see those values? In *prices* that we're willing to pay for different goods and services. Price is an expression of the desire of the purchaser to sell something and the desire of the consumer to purchase something.
E. But here's what that tells us about prices: there must be an agreement on price between sellers (supply) and buyers (demand) at a point in time when an exchange is made.

6. The constantly changing prices between these two groups is based on changes in supply and demand. This relationship is summarized in the Law of Supply and the Law of Demand.
   A. The Law of Demand states that consumers will purchase *more* of a good when its price decreases, but they will purchase *less* of a good when its price increases (all things being equal—in other words, assuming no other significant factor affects the choice to purchase). We see this all the time when a store puts an item on sale and people buy more of it than they would have at the normal price.
   B. The Law of Supply states that an increase in the price of a good means that there will eventually be an increase in the quantity of those goods produced by people. Again, we see this all the time when one company introduces a new product and charges a premium for it, then lots of other companies start producing the same or comparable products. They're just trying to get in on the action, but the increased supply means that unless demand is going up, the price will start to drop to find equilibrium.
   C. There are all sorts of ways these two factors relate to one another to adjust price. Here are four simple ones, the first two showing changes on the supply side and the second two showing changes on the demand side.
      i. Let's say the supply of apples goes up because there is a great crop. But the demand for apples does not change. As a result, the increased supply and unchanged demand means that the price of apples will drop since the sellers will want to entice more people to buy apples.

ii. The supply of apples goes down because there is a terrible crop. But the demand for apples does not change. As a result, the decreased supply and unchanged demand means that the price of apples will rise since the sellers have only so many apples and those people who want apples more than others will pay more to get them.
iii. Or, let's say that there is a new report that says apples help people lose weight. So the demand for apples increase, but the supply remains the same. As a result, the price of apples will increase so that those who really want the apples are the ones who will buy them.
iv. Finally, perhaps there is a report that says that apples are bad for you and eating too many causes health problems. As a result, the demand for apples goes down while the supply again remains the same. And so the price will drop to coax more people to buy apples.
v. In all these instances, the various value scales of individual consumers influenced the overall pricing of the market. But the market never sits still, especially if there is a growing market for a good.
vi. So, if the demand for apples is going up, and the price is also rising, then producers will plant more apple trees and produce more apples. At some point, these additional apples will satisfy the market and bring the prices back down to a lower point.

D. Prices are the result of a money system, showing us where supply and demand meet. Where those two things meet is called the *market price*—which is the fair price when it reflects what consumers are willing to pay and what producers are willing to sell for.

7. Although we've seen that what one values is different between two people, it's also true that one person values different amounts of the same things differently.
   A. We understand this very easily from our actions: although eating one bowl of ice cream may leave you wanting more, eating ten bowls of ice cream will leave you sick.
   B. The principle that explains this is called the *Law of Marginal Utility* (or diminishing marginal utility, because the usefulness of something goes down the more you have of it). By 'marginal' economists are referring to those things at the edges, and that the more of something you have, the less additional ones you'll want.
   C. For instance, you're hungry and eat an apple. When you finish, you will be less hungry than when you started, but you may still want to eat another. After eating the second apple, however, your hunger is satisfied even more, and so you may not be sure you want a third apple. You contemplate it, decide you'll try it, but after finishing it, you're really full. Therefore, when you're offered a forth apple, it actually turns your stomach. What happened in that short space of time? You lived out the law of marginal utility. Of course, this law applies to all economic goods and services, not just apples.
   D. This law, when applied to supply and demand, is actually a powerful force to stabilize prices. For instance,

if someone is buying apples for himself, and he knows he can only eat 5 to 6 in a week, he won't buy a bushel of 20 apples since he knows they'll go bad. Even if the price of 20 apples is just a bit higher than 5–6 apples, he still likely wouldn't buy it because the additional apples don't have any use for him; he knows he'd waste the money. So producers who are trying to sell their supply are forced to price things in a way that matches the buyer's usefulness, and they simply can't go too high or sell too many at one time.

8. All these supply and demand relationships concerning price and marginal utility are really just ways that God has structured free markets to meet the wants and needs of countless individuals in extremely efficient ways.
   A. After all, when the law of supply and demand are coupled together with things like free trade and mass production, we see that supplies go up and prices go down to provide for even the poorest members of a society. As Adam Smith realized, when goods and services are more plentiful and less expensive, then the purchasing power of the individual man or woman is greatly increased and their needs and wants more easily met. It has happened time and again in the West as an entire culture has grown more and more wealthy in comparison to the rest of the world.
   B. All of these economic relationships are built around men and women freely choosing what to do with their vocations, with their products, with their money, and with their markets. When men and women are given the ability to trade freely with one another from their surplus, they can more than meet the needs of each

other and overcome the natural scarcity and limitations in the current state of the created order.

C. We can easily see it by looking back over the past two hundred and fifty years. Since the founding of our nation, much time was spent following sound economic thinking and pursuing God-given liberty within laws reflecting His order.

D. Such liberty moves a people away from scarcity and puts them on the path to greater prosperity.

MULTIPLE CHOICE

1. ________ is an internal scale within each person that constantly changes based on a variety of things.
   a. Subjective judgment
   b. Economic value
   c. Economic worth
   d. Demand

2. A free market is when people enter into agreements ________.
   a. financially
   b. contractually
   c. voluntarily
   d. arbitrarily

3. ________ is an expression of the desire of the purchaser to sell something and the consumer to purchase something.
   a. Money
   b. Value
   c. Supply
   d. Price

4. The Law of Demand states that consumers will purchase _______ of a good when its price decreases, but they will purchase _______ of a good when its price increases.
   a. more.....less
   b. more.....more
   c. less.....more
   d. less.....less

5. The Law of Supply states that an _______ in the price of a good means that there will eventually be an _______ in the quantity of those goods produced by people.
   a. decrease.....decrease
   b. increase.....decrease
   c. decrease.....increase
   d. increase.....increase

SHORT ANSWER

1. How is the God-given scale of economic value important to our role as stewards in light of what God has given us?

2. Why is it important that money serve as a store of value in a market economy?

3. How is it that the laws of supply and demand rely on consistent and predictable human action?

4. Briefly explain the economic principles God has put in place to lead a society from scarcity to plenty? Can you cite real-world examples where you've seen this happen?

DISCUSSION

1. In a truly free market, is there ever something like an unfair price assuming a buyer and a seller voluntarily agree to it? What does this mean for us when we're shopping—do we ever really *have* to buy one thing, or do we always have a variety of options in the market, including the right not to buy at all?
2. Why is money so important to markets?
3. Markets can be large and small. Provide some personal examples of real experiences with a market that bears out the principles of supply and demand.
4. Some charitable organizations are interested in giving money and food to poorer nations; others are interested in teaching basic economics and providing economic means for wealth building. Why is it so important that these go together?

FOR FURTHER STUDY

Basic Economics, 3rd Ed.—Carson & Cleveland—Chapter 9

Prosperity and Poverty—Beisner—Chapter 8

Multiple choice answers: 1.b 2.c 3.d 4.a 5.d

5

The Role of the Entrepreneur: Capital, Calculation and Profit

MESSAGE INTRODUCTION

Individuals who seek to create new products or services are engines of economic growth. In this lesson, we will look at the entrepreneur; the role of capital in production; the importance of economic calculation; the source of jobs; the role of technology; serving consumers; competition and profit.

SCRIPTURE READING

Matthew 25—The Parable of the Talents

Luke 16—The Parable of the Dishonest Manager

LEARNING OBJECTIVES

1. To understand the role entrepreneurs play in the economy.
2. To see the importance of economic calculation to all economic decisions.
3. To recognize that profits are a key motivation for everyone selling in the marketplace.

QUOTATIONS

I never perfected an invention that I did not think about in terms of the service it might give others... I find out what the world needs, then I proceed to invent.

—Thomas Edison

Successful entrepreneurs, whatever their individual motivation...try to create value and to make a contribution.

—Peter Drucker

LECTURE OUTLINE

1. The entrepreneur is the one who makes the decision to bring a good or service into the marketplace.
   A. There is always a risk associated with such a decision. It requires the coordination of land, labor and capital in a particular way in the hopes that the product will be purchased by consumers. Entrepreneurs must speculate about what consumers will want in the future.
   B. Often the entrepreneur is considered to be a caricature of someone in a pinstriped suit, very fast moving and living in the big city. Although some entrepreneurs do look like that, the reality is that the majority of entrepreneurs are average men and women who have an idea, start a company, then work very hard to bring a product to market and make their business successful.

2. An entrepreneur will need lots of things to be able to create a new product and successfully sell it.
   A. One of the first things an entrepreneur needs is *capital*. He or she can get that capital either by saving or by borrowing. Remember that capital goods are any

number of things that are used to create other things, with money being one of the most common forms of capital. However, tools are another important type of capital, and they will differ depending on the particular needs of each business.

B. The next thing the entrepreneur will need is accurate information. This includes pricing information, the elements and costs of creating the new product, the potential size of the market (number of customers), the necessary tools, and so on and so forth. The entrepreneur will then need to make a lot of calculated decisions based on the information he has at hand. This process of gathering information and then making decisions (such as comparing revenue with costs) is referred to as *economic calculation.*

C. One of those decisions is whether the entrepreneur should hire someone or not. If he does choose to hire someone, then he is creating one new job for the economy. Jobs come from businesses and businesses come from entrepreneurs. All the private-sector jobs that are out there, whether months or centuries old, ultimately had their start in an entrepreneur's vision and hard work.

D. The entrepreneur makes an agreement with those who work for him: he will trade a certain amount of money for that person's labor. Essentially, every time someone earns a paycheck, they are making a trade for their labor. This is why the entrepreneur ultimately owns what comes from the labor's work: he has contracted to trade something the laborer values more than his work: a paycheck.

E. This means that all consumers are receiving their money from some entrepreneurial source, whether they work directly for a business or are being supported through the redistribution of wealth from those working in businesses (i.e., a government job). At the end of the day, we are all both consumers and producers since we are both producing things and purchasing things.

3. Another important part of an entrepreneur's economic calculation is locating and applying the proper *technology* to his business.
   A. Entrepreneurs are constantly thinking about investing in those tools that will increase their workers' productivity, or lower the costs for production, or enable their products to be better, or get to market faster. All of these things (and more) go into the application of technology.
   B. What is the source of modern technology? It comes from a Christian understanding of the world. Many of the technologies that we rely on today have their roots in the medieval and Renaissance periods. These were times when the dominant Christian worldview saw the world as ordered, rational, and dependable, thus enabling modern science to grow up beneath its tutelage. A Christian view of science, when combined with free markets, created the unique technological impetus first seen in the Western world for the rapid development of new technology.
   C. Furthermore, the principle of private property is very important to technology. The possibility of owning what one creates is a strong motivation to figure out new and unusual things that can be sold. After all, if

you don't own what you create, then there's far less incentive to figure out new technologies.

D. We see this motivation throughout the early history of America, where men like Cyrus McCormack, Alexander Graham Bell, Thomas Edison, and others changed the world with their inventions. As a result, America leaped over many European nations to enter the 20th century as one of the most technologically advanced and prosperous nations in the world. This growth and prosperity was all grounded in a Christian worldview.

E. But without the free market as a strong motivator, it's likely none of these inventions would have happened, much less spread with such speed. Technological process is not innate and natural; rather, it comes from a unique relationship between entrepreneurs and consumers where discovery and the pursuit of new ideas are financially rewarded within the free market.

4. Finally, an entrepreneur must know how to manage his capital well to create a new product. This is where prices denominated in money are very useful.
   A. Money prices enable an entrepreneur to measure costs and plan for the future.
   B. Prices enable him to know what it will cost to get the land, the labor, and the capital to create a new product.
   C. Prices also show him that he can't sell below his own costs, otherwise he will quickly go bankrupt.
   D. Finally, prices enable an entrepreneur to look into a particular market and see what similar items sell for, thereby helping him determine his own prices.

5. Who is the entrepreneur really serving in the marketplace? The consumer.

A. The entrepreneur desires to bring his product to a market and have consumers voluntarily exchange their money for what he is selling. He can only be successful within the free market if he is meeting the desires of the consumer.
B. Put another way, the entrepreneur is gathering together the means of production, he is coordinating them, he is working hard, for the simple reason of meeting some need or desire of a consumer. Why is he doing this? What motivates the entrepreneur to go into the service of the consumer?
C. One of the primary motivations for the entrepreneur is his desire for *profit*. What is profit? Profit is what is left over after the entrepreneur takes into account all of his costs in creating his product and bringing it to market to sell. Now, there are a lot of costs involved in this process, but if it sells for more than these costs, then that's a profit.
D. Today, some people talk about profits as if there's something wrong with them, especially if they consider them to be high. But here's what's interesting: those people are normally talking about *someone else's* profits, not their own. They never have a profit that's too high—just the guy they read about in the paper. This is one of the reasons for the 10th Commandment: do not covet.
E. But if profits are made freely through trades within the free market, then they really can never be too high. The reason is this: if millions of people willingly decide to exchange their money for a new brand of cell phone, no one is coercing them to make that trade.

They are voluntarily giving someone else their money in exchange for what they want more. And that's a good thing. Of course, the company on the other end of the trade makes enormous profits. But those profits are perfectly legitimate and fair.

F. Furthermore, profits are a reward to the entrepreneur for the risk he took in creating that new product and bringing it to market. And there are certainly great risks to being an entrepreneur! It's estimated that two-thirds of the businesses that start every year will be closed within three years. That can mean lost savings, lost homes, and bankruptcies. Furthermore, those people who were unhappy about others making huge profits are normally not interested in helping offset huge losses.

G. This is why entrepreneurs need a strong motivation to be entrepreneurial; that motivation is the opportunity for profit. If you take that away, you take away the motive that creates the products, you take away the products that create the jobs, and you take away the jobs that create income. Any entrepreneur who is willing to take great risks to start a business is certainly worthy of great rewards.

H. Is this fair? Yes, because consumers are voting with their own money. Ultimately, entrepreneurs are a great help to consumers in meeting their wants and needs with new products. But entrepreneurs are also a great help to consumers when more than one enters the same market.

6. Competition between entrepreneurs and their products is one of the strongest forces unleashed by the free market.

A. When one entrepreneur makes a great profit selling or doing something, this alerts other entrepreneurs that there is an opportunity for them also to make a profit.
B. Remember our discussion in lesson 4 about the laws of supply and demand, and that a growing demand will mean that supplies will increase to meet that demand. Entrepreneurs are the ones who take the risk to increase a supply in a market.
C. One of the ways entrepreneurs will compete is in the pricing of their products. In other words, each will try to sell lower than the other if he can. This process normally requires entrepreneurs to be clever in how they coordinate the factors of production, saving here and there so they can transfer that to their prices.
D. What does this mean to the consumer? All things being equal, prices on most products have a tendency to go down over time. Think about the computer industry: competition keeps prices low and enables more and more consumers to buy more and more of the goods they want for less money.
E. Another thing competition encourages is product improvement. Entrepreneurs know that if they can make an improvement or adjustment in a product, they may not have to lower the price but can offer something better than the competition to a consumer. Again, the consumer wins in the struggle between entrepreneurs trying to make a profit.

7. Profit is therefore the economic force driving the growth of the free market. It is one more economic principle that has brought prosperity to the West like the world has

never seen before. We often don't realize it because we're living in the middle of it.

A. But if we compare the lives of the richest men and kings from just 200 years ago, we realize that how they lived their lives, the goods and services at their disposal, and the comforts they enjoyed were not the equal of the average man or woman living in the West today. This is a fascinating and remarkable situation, one that the rest of the world has looked at in hopes of trying to follow in our footsteps.

B. How did we get here? It was because the men and women of the West began to live in the light of the way God made us. We started to harness the principles that God created to grow an economy. And those in the West realized that the path to prosperity is in turning everyone's self-interest into the service of others.

C. When this happens in the context of a society, that society prospers. When it happens in the context of a nation, there is national prosperity.

8. This brings us back to the solution of our initial question: who decides what to produce and how much, and who decides what to consume and how much? In a free market system, everybody decides.

A. In talking about the free market, Adam Smith spoke of the idea of an 'invisible hand' that guided markets to a good outcome. He gave us this image to say that God worked in and around and through market systems to oversee and control all things.

B. But the reality is that this image can be misleading. God controls all things, not just markets. Furthermore, God works through means; or in this case, individual people.

C. After all, God designed each and every one of us to be rational, to be purposeful, to have the ability to choose, to be able to cooperate and exchange. It is therefore in our very being to seek out and create markets, to act with self-interest, and to need to serve one another. The reason free markets work so very well and have always worked so well is that God designed us to naturally prosper within them. It is simply a result of being made in the image of God.

MULTIPLE CHOICE

1. _______ : used to create other things, with money being one of the most common forms.
   a. Tools
   b. Capital
   c. Trade
   d. Production

2. The process of gathering information and then making decisions is referred to as _______.
   a. economic calculation
   b. investment analysis
   c. monetary management
   d. fiscal insight

3. _______ is what is left over after the entrepreneur takes into account his costs in creating his product and bringing his product to market to sell it.
   a. Residual income
   b. Revenue
   c. Profit
   d. Money

4. _______ between entrepreneurs and their products is one of the strongest forces unleashed by the free market.
   a. Interaction
   b. Income
   c. Derivatives
   d. Competition

5. The path to prosperity is in turning everyone's _______ into the service of others.
   a. self-interest
   b. welfare
   c. value judgments
   d. stewardship

SHORT ANSWER

1. Explain the process of entrepreneurialism step-by-step. How is this similar and different from the way God creates?

2. Choose an example of technology from history, look up the entrepreneur behind it, and explain what it has done for society. How has it made society better?

3. Why is there such a negative attitude toward profit in our society today? What does that mean for the growth of the economy long term?

DISCUSSION

1. Think about the first chapter of Genesis and compare ways that the entrepreneur is simply following in God's footsteps with what he does.
2. List out a variety of different markets you've experienced, then explain how (and why) they work.
3. What does it mean that 'God designed us to naturally prosper within markets?' How does this fit with what you know of the way man was created?
4. Sometimes people are critical of all the "stuff" available in a free society. Yet would producers be producing these things if someone wasn't buying them? Is this a reflection of the free market, or a reflection of the people making up society at that moment? If we look in the garages, rooms, and drawers in our homes, is there a lot of stuff in them? If that bothers us, whose fault is it: the seller or the buyer?
5. What are ways that entrepreneurialism can be married to missions? To local ministries always in need of support? To training of foreign national Christians? Are there ways for groups to be "tent-building" ministries instead of simply receiving donations?

FOR FURTHER STUDY

Basic Economics, 3rd Ed.—Carson & Cleveland—Chapters 11–12
Foundations of Economics—Ritenour—Chapters 5–6

Multiple choice answers: 1.b 2.a 3.c 4.d 5.a

6

A Tale of Two Theologies, Part 1: From God to Politics

MESSAGE INTRODUCTION

Theological ideas have far-reaching consequences, including both political and economic systems. In this lesson, we'll look at the competing worldviews of Christianity and Atheism; at how philosophy, theology, and economics are related; at Theology, or one's view of God; at Anthropology, or one's view of Man; at Political Philosophy; and at Political Systems.

SCRIPTURE READING

Psalm 2

Daniel 2

LEARNING OBJECTIVES

1. To understand there are two kingdoms and two worldviews struggling against each other, each of which seeks to control all aspects of a society.
2. To see the connections between theology, anthropology, political philosophy and political systems.
3. To recognize that free markets, political liberty, and freedom to worship God are all interconnected.

QUOTATIONS

> *Its view of God, its knowledge of God, its experience of God, is what alone gives character to a society or nation, and meaning to its destiny. Its culture, the voice of this character, is merely that view, knowledge, experience of God, fixed by its most intense spirits in terms intelligible to the mass of men. There has never been a society or nation without God. But history is cluttered with the wreckage of nations that became indifferent to God, and died.*
>
> —Whitaker Chambers, *Witness*

LECTURE OUTLINE

1. Almost everyone is familiar with the concept 'ideas have consequences.' It is also important to realize that there are consequences to economic ideas.
   A. Some people are skeptical of this perspective, and instead think that economics is separate from the rest of our lives.
   B. If it is true, however, that economics is intimately related to the cultural mandate and our being stewards under God, then economics is related to many other things, including our philosophy and our theology. The results of our beliefs about economics therefore have profound consequences to our lives as stewards under God.
   C. We can demonstrate this by comparing two nations that followed two very different economic systems at different times in history:
      i. To begin with, England (and all of Great Britain) in the late eighteenth and nineteenth centuries can be held up as one of the best

examples of a free market economy. From the 1750's forward, we see the full flowering of the industrial revolution occurring on this small island, as well as the wisdom of Adam Smith being published in the *Wealth of Nations*.

1. At the same time in Britain, we see the commencement of the modern missionary movement with the sending of William Carey to India in 1793. During the 19th-century and beyond, England, Scotland, Wales & Ireland sent out thousands of missionaries to places like China, India, Africa, Australia, New Zealand, and other countries in order to share the good news of Jesus Christ. Each of these missionaries was financed by the surplus savings of average men and women living in Great Britain.
2. The work of these missionaries ultimately resulted in the conversion of hundreds of millions of people and was the primary reason the gospel can be found in many of these countries today.

ii. In comparison, look at the history of Russia in the twentieth century. In 1917, a communist socialist economy based on the ideas of Karl Marx was established under the leadership of Vladimir Lenin. It was called the Union of Soviet Socialist Republics, or, for short, the Soviet Union.

1. What happened to Christians in the Soviet Union? Any foreign missionaries were expelled and the millions of Christians living in the country began to be perse-

cuted, so much so that from 1917 to 1980, approximately 24 million Christians met their deaths at the hands of this communist socialist state. Tens of thousands of churches were destroyed, hundreds of thousands of children were separated from their parents, and millions of men and women were sent to the Soviet prisons.

2. Yet such persecution of Christians was not unique to the Soviet Union. Many other socialist countries have persecuted Christians: it happened in Nazi Germany, it happened in Cambodia; and it happens to this day in Vietnam, in Cuba, in North Korea, and in China.

D. Why is this? Why would there be such is a strong connection between a society's rejection of market systems and its need to imprison Christians and put them to death? That is what this lesson and the following lesson are all about: exploring the worldviews that are in conflict with one another and that work themselves out in specific economic systems.

E. The point of this contrast, however, is extremely clear. Not just England, but those other nations God has blessed with free markets and liberty have been those nations that have sent out and financed the modern missionary movement, bringing untold millions of people into the Kingdom of God. And not just the Soviet Union, but other nations which have fully embraced a socialist economy have oppressed and murdered Christians all across the globe. Economic ideas do have consequences, far beyond what is in our bank accounts.

F. Ultimately, though, these temporal battles are just the outworking of the real battle in the world between the Kingdom of God and the kingdom of Satan. We must not miss the truth that economics plays a very important role in the intense struggle over who will control the world. *Now war arose in heaven, Michael and his angels fighting against the dragon. And the dragon and his angels fought back, but he was defeated, and there was no longer any place for them in heaven. And the great dragon was thrown down, that ancient serpent, who is called the devil and Satan, the deceiver of the whole world—he was thrown down to the earth, and his angels were thrown down with him* (Rev. 12:7–9).

2. In Lesson 2, we introduced a metaphor that illustrates how economics is influenced by our worldview.
   A. We said:
      i. Theology, or the study of God
      ii. Leads to believing certain things about man, or Anthropology
      iii. Which in turn informs a Political Philosophy
      iv. Which leads to a Political System,
      v. Which helps determine an Economic Philosophy
      vi. Which manifests itself in an Economic System.
   B. Now, it's true that this is just a simplification of a rather complex set of interrelationships, but it does provide a picture of how one idea intersects and then influences a related idea. Most importantly, however, it shows how all the ideas that affect our daily lives can be traced back to what we believe about God and man.

C. Our objective in these next two lessons is to compare two competing worldviews that have had a dominant influence in the modern world: a Christian and an Atheistic worldview. These worldviews are nothing less than the outworking of the two different kingdoms doing battle in the world.

3. To begin with, let's compare the *Theology*, or the views of God, between these two systems. It may seem odd to speak about an atheistic theology, but the fact is that even those who deny the reality of the God of the Bible must have beliefs that take His place, since He is foundational to everything that exists.
   A. Sovereignty
      i. From a Christian perspective, God is sovereign, transcendent and all-powerful. He rules over all of creation and everything else is beneath Him.
      ii. From the atheist perspective, because there is no God, man is the highest order of being and so is elevated to the highest authority in the universe. Man himself must fill the vacuum he has created by removing God, and so in the atheistic system, Man is God.
   B. Purpose and History
      i. Christians believe that because God is sovereign and transcendent, He is moving mankind in a particular direction though history. God is governing the events that happen in the universe and He is moving the world to a place where all His glory will be known. The goal of history is to glorify Himself through the ever-expanding reign of Jesus Christ over all creation.

ii. On the other hand, atheists believe at least two things concerning the governance and history of the world:
    1. Some believe that history is random and that we're not going anywhere; or, if not exactly random, then perhaps it is cyclical and we're all doomed to repeat what has happened before. Either view is devoid of any real direction or order.
    2. Others believe that history is going somewhere, not guided by God but by the work and efforts of Man. These believe in some form of future utopia (or worker's paradise, as taught by Karl Marx) where mankind is better as a result of evolution and self-improvement.

C. The Creation or Natural Order
  i. When Christians affirm that God is sovereign and transcendent, they also affirm that He has a relationship to the creation that is personal and immanent. He does not just sit above creation, but involves Himself within it in a personal, relational way. He therefore made man to interact with Him on a spiritual level. This means that not only is there a physical realm, but there is also a spiritual, supernatural realm that is an integrated part of the created order. *And they heard the sound of the LORD God walking in the garden in the cool of the day....But the LORD God called to the man and said to him, "Where are you?"* (Gen. 3:8–9).

ii. From the atheist's perspective, however, the physical universe that we see, hear, taste and touch is all that there is. The material universe is sometimes called by atheists a closed system; it is uncreated and eternal itself, without a spiritual realm beyond it.

4. In talking about Theology, we inevitably begin to talk about *Anthropology*, or the view of man. This level includes a wide variety of concepts, such as:
   A. Man's Nature
      i. Christians teach that man is made in the image of God with an eternal soul. Because we are made in His image, we have dignity, we have eternal worth, we have unique abilities and callings. We are rational, we have purpose, and we have the ability to make choices. Ultimately, our natures are designed to bear God's image and to do the work of stewards fulfilling the cultural mandate. *Yet you have made him a little lower than the heavenly beings and crowned him with glory and honor. You have given him dominion over the works of your hands; you have put all things under his feet* (Ps. 8:5–6).
      ii. In the atheist worldview, man is the byproduct of cosmic chance. There is nothing eternally dignified or worthwhile to man other than what he himself determines. Man has no eternal soul made in the image of God, and so simply returns to the dust from which he came. Yet, often the atheist worldview argues inconsistently that even though we arose by chance and our lives

will end in nothingness, we can have dignity, purpose and grandeur in the time in between.

B. Work
   i. As we've looked at previously, the Christian teaches that man was designed to be a steward of God's creation and that work is a blessing, a gift, and a privilege. Our work is ultimately done in service to God. *Commit your work to the LORD, and your plans will be established* (Prov. 16:3).
   ii. In the atheistic perspective, man is an end unto himself. He must determine his own purposes for his work, whether practical or philosophical. Without some divine purpose, a society eventually begins to question the innate value in work, and members of society try either to avoid it or to have someone else do it for them.

C. Family
   i. In Genesis, we see God's stewardship call to work given in the context of families: *And God said to them, "Be fruitful and multiply and fill the earth..."* (Gen. 1:28). The growth and multiplication of countless families consisting of a man and a woman, their children, and their children's children, is the pattern of global stewardship for the Christian.
   ii. For the atheist, however, the family is just a social construct that can be freely taken apart and rebuilt at will depending on the desires or purposes of other men. The family has no lasting definition and purpose beyond that of man's own designs.

D. Purpose
   i. The Christian states that man's ultimate purpose is to worship God, both individually and communally.
   ii. The atheist, on the other hand, was designed for worship, but denies the existence of the eternal God for whom he was made. As a result, he ends up worshipping some part of the creation, just as Paul tells us in Romans 1: *For although they knew God, they did not honor him as God or give thanks to him, but they became futile in their thinking...and exchanged the glory of the immortal God for images resembling mortal man and birds and animals and creeping things* (Rom. 1:21–23).
E. Moral Condition
   i. The Christian affirms that Man is fundamentally sinful and in rebellion against God. He has a sin nature that makes him basically fallible. Left to his own devices, he will seek to dominate and control other men. *All have turned aside; together they have become worthless; no one does good, not even one* (Rom. 3:12).
   ii. The atheist argues against this by saying Man is basically good and morally upright. His primary problem is not a broken nature, but a lack of education. Man is infinitely malleable by other men; if he can only be properly instructed, he can rise above his brothers to a higher moral level.
   iii. This seems to be a grand irony: the Christian worldview says man is made in God's image, yet

is severely broken; the atheist worldview says that Man comes from chance and dust, yet is eminently perfectible.

iv. Of course, if there is any Christian doctrine that has abundant historical evidence, it is the sinfulness of man. The twentieth century alone has proven beyond a shadow of a doubt that the only thing Man has perfected is the ability to control and destroy other men.

5. Understanding the basic points of these two competing worldviews should help explain how a culture forms its *political philosophy,* or the intellectual framework that informs a society's government and laws.
   A. Freedom to Worship
      i. A political philosophy based on a Christian worldview establishes freedom of worship as the first and most important right of a people. We see this in the two most famous documents expressing a political philosophy based on a Christian worldview:
         1. England's Magna Carta states at the beginning that: "In the first place we have granted to God, and by this our present charter confirmed for us and our heirs forever that the English Church shall be free, and shall have her rights entire, and her liberties inviolate." (Magna Carta, 1215)
         2. The First Amendment to the US Constitution states: "Congress shall make no law respecting an establishment of religion, or prohibiting the free exercise thereof."

ii. Under an atheist system, however, there can be no freedom to worship God since the goal is for man to worship the State.
   1. Immediately after its formation in 1917, the Soviet Union passed a series of Acts and Decrees that broke apart the structure of the Christian church in Russia, shut down many churches, and forbade most Christian activities. This philosophy of oppression continued throughout the existence of the Soviet Union.
   2. The atheist State's "deification" of its central leaders, however, can be seen in their ubiquitous portraits everywhere throughout socialist countries.

B. Source of Law
   i. In a Christian system, political laws are supposed to reflect the very laws that God Himself has revealed to us. Human law is to reflect divine law in the same way that human beings are a reflection of God's being.
   ii. In an atheistic system, because man considers himself to be God, all the laws are grounded in the unsafe place of a few men's wills. There is no external source of law: all laws are man-made. As a result, this quickly consolidates itself into a few people, either the brighter or the more powerful, who then impose their wills on the rest of society.

C. Liberty and Freedom
   i. According to the Christian worldview, liberty and freedom are necessary for us to do our work

as economic stewards before God. Personal liberty is vitally important to a Christian political philosophy because it creates the space within which a society can grow and prosper.

ii. According to the atheist worldview, however, liberty and freedom are redefined as that which is best for the State. In this system, the State does not exist to support its citizens, but the citizens exist to support the State.

D. Power of the Sword

i. A Christian political philosophy sees the police and military powers of the State being used as minimally as possible. Their primary purpose is to protect us from aggressors, foreign and domestic. The function of the sword is to fight off all who would oppress us.

ii. In the atheistic system, the sword is taken up by the State for the direct purpose of oppressing its citizens. Because the State feels the compelling need to use its power to remake and reshape its citizens, the sword becomes something that wounds them rather than protecting them.

E. Distribution of Power

i. The Christian view starts off with the fact that all men are sinners, including those running the government. As result, the government itself needs to be kept in check, so a series of checks and balances are developed where one part of the government is restrained by another part.

ii. The atheistic view, however, doesn't see men as sinful. The result? Power is purposely centralized and focused in one place, so that the State can be controlled by a small body of people (or just one person).

F. Centralization
    i. The Christian system pushes toward decentralization. Individual liberty is held to be most important, where each of us can make our own decisions concerning our own lives and the lives of our families.
    ii. In the atheist system, they push toward more centralization where individual liberty is irrelevant, and where a central power can make decisions concerning the lives of its people and families.

6. A political philosophy is worked out in a real *political system*. This is the actual structure of a government in the context of a nation.
    A. Constitutions
        i. In a Christian political system, the rule of law is of primary importance. As a result, these countries will establish written constitutions that reside above everyone. The best constitutions are difficult to change, but are amendable if necessary. Above all, they put the laws in written form so everyone can see and know that they are not being made up based on someone's whims. This is a reflection of how God put His laws in writing and publicized them for all to know and see.
        ii. In an atheistic political system, the laws are easy to change since they reside in the wills of just a few people or one person. Whether it's an individual totalitarian regime, an oligarchy, or

some cabal of leaders, there is no document that can be referred to by the people to hold those leaders accountable.

B. Selection of Leaders
    i. It is important to choose good leaders to run the political system. But how to choose them? A Christian worldview involves local voting and representation. Leaders are chosen by the people to apply the laws already written down, or to pass new ones. Leaders must work within the restrictions of what the constitution allows.
    ii. In an atheistic system, leaders historically get into power through intrigues, coups, and assassinations. There is no succession plan; instead, the strongest normally ends up with the reigns of power.
C. Police
    i. From a Christian perspective, police are necessary to protect life and property. But in a moral society, it should be a limited job; even in a society with moral breakdown, the police are only there to protect and not to coerce. The goal is a police force that is small but effective.
    ii. From an atheist perspective, however, the police grow large since they are the primary arm for coercing citizens to do the will of the leaders. Police powers balloon in an atheist political system, with more and more armed guards being brought in to control the lives of citizens.
D. Education
    i. In a Christian system, education is the responsibility of parents, not the State. The Christian worldview sees education as a family function,

not that of government. As a result, a Christian political system gives liberty and freedom to parents in this regard.

ii. In contrast to this, an atheist system desires to shape its people through the use of education. There is real necessity for centralized, government run schools where the youngest members of the culture can be instructed and trained in the service of the State.

7. After seeing how these four areas build on each other with significant consequences for the way people live and act, is it not to be expected that there will be as great a contrast in the realm of economics?
   A. If the atheist worldview wants to deny freedom of worship, control education, and police its people, how do you think that will affect economics?
   B. Won't there also be a desire to control labor and the fruits of labor? Won't there be a system to control choices, purchasing, and the development of a controlled economy?
   C. In the same way, won't the Christian system emphasize economic freedoms and liberty in order to give men and women the ability to be effective stewards under God?

MULTIPLE CHOICE

1. All the ideas that affect our daily lives can be traced back to what we believe about ________.
   a. Economics and money
   b. Philosophy and knowledge
   c. God and man
   d. Thinking and reason

2. Christians believe that because God is ________, He is moving mankind in a particular direction though history.
   a. loving and wise
   b. sovereign and transcendent
   c. generous and great
   d. holy and powerful

3. The study of man is called ________.
   a. ontology
   b. epistemology
   c. anthropology
   d. teleology

4. A political philosophy is the intellectual framework that informs a society's ________.
   a. government and laws
   b. economy and policies
   c. prestige and reputation
   d. structure and worldview

5. In a Christian political system, the rule of law is of primary importance. As a result, these countries will establish ________ that sit above everyone.
   a. judicial courts
   b. elected presidencies
   c. voting parliaments
   d. written constitutions

SHORT ANSWER

1. Explain how some of the premises of an atheistic theology lead to an atheistic political system.

2. Why does a Christian worldview lead to written constitutions and an atheistic worldview lead to centralized leaders?

3. Compare and contrast the way leaders are chosen in the two systems and how this is reflective of different times in Israel's history.

DISCUSSION

1. Talking about worldviews in a black and white way like this may concern some people, but is it an accurate picture of what the Bible teaches? Name some other places where this concept is borne out Biblically.
2. Why do you think it's necessary for socialist countries to oppress Christians?
3. Why do you think that both founding documents include freedom of religion as their first comment?
4. Compare some political philosophies and systems of real countries in regard to liberty and tyranny.

FOR FURTHER STUDY

Economics: Principles and Policies—Rose—Chapter 4

Multiple choice answers: 1.c 2.b 3.c 4.a 5.d

7

A Tale of Two Theologies, Part 2: Economic Philosophies and Systems

MESSAGE INTRODUCTION

An economic philosophy and system should enable men and women to be effective stewards before God. In this lesson, we'll look at a 'North Star' Principle concerning stewardship; at the spectrum of economic systems; at two economic philosophies; at a comparison of economic systems, including free market, interventionist, and socialistic; at four basic economic questions; and at the different answers to those questions from free market, interventionist, and socialist economies.

SCRIPTURE READING

Exodus 5–6

LEARNING OBJECTIVES

1. To understand how to judge an economic system on the basis of how it affects man's ability to be a steward.
2. To see how economic philosophies ultimately come down to who has control of economic goods.
3. To recognize the distinctions between free market, interventionist, and socialist economies.

QUOTATIONS

> *It should be obvious that the natural outgrowth of civil government, if one takes the humanist viewpoint, is ultimately a controlled and regimented society: socialism, fascism, communism and the modern "welfare" state are different not in essence, but only in degree. In nations all over the world, man has produced economic systems that are politically controlled in place of economies that are free. This process has been going on even in these United States of America.*
>
> —Tom Rose, *Economics: Principles and Policy*

LECTURE OUTLINE

1. Introduction—A "North Star" Principle for Economics
   - A. Stewardship Logic
     - i. In this lesson, we'll carry our worldview comparison through the two final steps of economic philosophies and economic systems.
     - ii. First, let's introduce a "North Star" principle. When you start talking about economic philosophies and systems, it can quickly become complex. Here's a question we can ask that will clarify our thinking: how does an economic choice affect man's ability to be a God-obeying steward of creation? Does this economic system or policy enable men to be *better* stewards before God in fulfilling the cultural mandate, or does it *prevent* them and make fulfilling the cultural mandate difficult or even impossible?

iii. We saw in our first lesson that God owns everything, but that He has given different parts of the creation to individual men and women to steward in accordance with their unique skills and vocations. A 'stewardship logic' is the key to economics; it will be our north star that guides us through the second half of the course.

B. Our Adversaries

i. Satan, of course, does not want anyone to be a good steward of God's creation. This was his purpose in tempting Eve, and it continues to be his purpose as he misleads even well-meaning people into dysfunctional and anti-Christian economic systems.

ii. We know that there are only two groups in the world: those in the Kingdom of God and those in the kingdom of Satan. As a result, we also know that every individual—whether consciously or unconsciously—is working to build up God's kingdom or working to build up Satan's kingdom. One group is working to be stewards before God; the other is working to prevent them from being stewards. It is the struggle between these two kingdoms that explains all of world history, as well as the different political and economic systems that currently exist.

iii. Yet, it's not just Satan against us. We also can't forget the extraordinary impact of sin on the world. Sin affects everything. And because of sin, a completely free and truly Christian economic system can never be perfectly realized.

iv. On the other hand, those who strive to rid society of Christian principles face another problem. Because God has made the world to work in a certain way according to certain laws, a controlled, atheistic system also can never be completely realized. Denying basic economics over the long run is like trying to deny basic geometry—the world just doesn't work that way.

C. As a result, modern economic and political systems all fall somewhere on a spectrum between Christian and Atheistic political systems and economies. In fact, since man is a creature of time, there is a dynamism or growth to all these systems as Satan struggles to push man toward more atheism and control while God guides man toward more freedom under His law. It is a complex give and take, but as a society embraces God's design for its politics and economics, it will eventually prosper and thrive; as it rejects God's design for its politics and economics, it will eventually grow poor and decline.

2. By *economic philosophy*, we mean the theoretical thinking that supports any economic system.

A. The first and primary question of economic philosophy has to do with *Ownership*.

i. This parallels our first principle from our first lesson: God owns everything. He has fashioned the world in a purposeful way. He made man in His image to own certain parts of the world, and desires him to fashion those parts in a purposeful way. Ultimately, man can only steward what he owns.

ii. In a Christian economic system, individuals must have ownership of different parts of creation. In economic terms, we have referred to this ownership as *private property*. Just as God owns the entire world and can do whatever He wants with it, when one truly owns land, labor and capital, one has the right and ability to do what one wants with it under the guidance of God's law. You can most effectively steward what you own. Private ownership of property, therefore, is the foundation of a Christian economic philosophy.

iii. In an atheistic system, however, there is a complete denial of private property. The State owns everything. Those people running the State may allow individuals the use of certain things, but individuals do not ultimately own or control the means of production. The denial of private ownership of property is the hallmark of a non-Christian economic philosophy. Just think: if Satan can keep a man from owning anything, isn't it easier to keep him from being a steward?

B. What are some basic consequences of ownership? The first is *control.*

i. In a Christian system, because man can truly own property, final control of that property is left in his hands. God has given land, labor and capital to each according to His providential design. What we have, we must be able to control.

ii. Think of the story in Acts of Ananias and Sapphira who sold their land, but gave only part of the proceeds to the church. When asked about it, however, they said they had given all of it. Peter expressly declares that they had ownership and control of the property, which is the primary reason they are held responsible for their sin. He said: *"While it remained unsold, did it not remain your own? And after it was sold, was it not at your disposal?"* (Acts 5:4). Ownership always includes control.

iii. In an atheistic system, however, individual men do not ultimately control property since they don't own it. Property is instead controlled by the State, or those handful of men who control the State. Individual men can't even control their own labor since they work for the State. Since ownership and control are ultimately related, denying men control of creation prevents them from being Biblical stewards.

C. The second consequence of ownership is *purpose*.

i. In a Christian system, man is able to fulfill the cultural mandate by freely making choices as to what he should do with what he owns. His economic actions have certain goals that he himself sets.

a. He can pursue any *vocation* because he is free to follow the skills God gave him. If he wants to be a farmer, he can choose to plant wheat or beans or oranges or apples. If he wants to be a real estate developer, he can choose to build a skyscraper or a grocery store or a hospital or a house. He is free to do as he individually purposes. That purpose, however, must be guided by God's law and intentions for man.

b. He also has the *freedom to trade* with others to provide for his family, his church, and his business. His work through free trade (whether it's being paid for his labor or his products) enables him to support his family; this is a primary goal of man's economic actions. Another goal is support of the church and its ministries.

ii. In an atheistic system, the State determines the purposes man will have with any land, labor or capital.

a. Individual purpose is subsumed within the State's goals, therefore there can be no true freedom to trade.

b. Laws will be passed that will intentionally enable immoral activities to flourish, such as abortion clinics, gambling, or the pornography industry; laws will be passed that will oppress the church; and laws will target honest businesses either driving them out of business, or giving dishonest competitors government monopolies or subsidies since those businesses are supporting the government.

c. At the end of the day, economic support of the State is the primary purpose of man's economic actions and all his work must be dedicated to it.

D. We come now to an intersection between politics and economics. If one is to have ownership, control and purpose, if one is to have freedom to trade, then those things need to be affirmed and protected through *Law and Government*. Politics and economics are inseparably intertwined.

i. In Christian economic philosophy, the law exists to protect private property; the government is given the sword to enforce its protection.

a. Because of sin, people will covet what others have and seek different ways to take their property from them.

b. Laws are therefore designed to protect private property and enable man to be a better steward. They protect the economic support of the family; they protect the church; they protect man's right to own, control, and freely purpose his land, labor and capital. In other words, in a Christian economic philosophy, the law and government are there to support man's stewardship activities.

ii. But this is exactly the opposite in an atheistic system. There the law exists to protect state property and the government rules over the people to control their actions. There are not laws protecting the family, the church, and the individual's right to own, control, and purpose his property. Instead, the law becomes a means of economic oppression and control.

E. What does this all come down to? What does our stewardship logic show us? Economic philosophies can all be reduced to the question of 'who has ultimate control of economic goods?'

i. In a Christian philosophy, the individual acts as steward before God and has only God's law as his guiding and controlling factor. There are no other individuals who control his economic actions. He has freedom to own, control, and trade his goods according to his own purposes.

ii. In an atheistic philosophy, however, some small group of individuals works to control the actions of all other individuals in accordance with their own purposes and goals.

iii. There's no getting away from the principle of ownership of property: it's a fact of creation. The question, rather, is *who* owns it? *Who* controls it? *Who* purposes it?

3. As we move to our final step, we see that an *economic system* is the real outworking of an economic philosophy. It is enabled or enforced by the laws of the state. But, just as real political systems are messy and inconsistent because implemented by sinners, so, too, are real economic systems.

   A. There is a spectrum of economic systems that stretch between two poles generally corresponding to the poles of Christian and Atheistic economic philosophy:

      i. On one side are *free market* economies.

      ii. On the other side are *socialist,* or *command & control* economies.

      iii. Almost all modern economies fall somewhere on the spectrum between these two extremes. Furthermore, economies are dynamic, and always moving in one of these two directions: either toward greater individual economic freedom or toward greater centralized economic control.

iv. Economies are complex. There are billions of people making decisions every second of every day in all the economies of the world. How can we understand these different systems and make a comparison simple? What we'll see is that everything comes down to how a particular system views and treats property, markets and law.
v. We explained in our first six lessons that God made man to work in a certain way under certain economic laws and principles, whether it be self-interest, vocation, division of labor, prices, production and consumption, and so forth. Markets are a key manifestation of how man was created to act.
vi. But throughout time, sinful people have realized that if it could somehow control or influence a particular market, they could better accomplish their own economic goals.
    a. For instance, at a national level, Pharaoh enslaved the people of Israel, thereby absolutely controlling their labor. They built entire cities for no remuneration and without any choice. (This is one of the reasons God had the Israelites ask their neighbors for gold, silver and jewels the day before the exodus—it was not robbery, but part of the pay they were owed for countless years of slavery.)
    b. At a local level, a merchant might use inaccurate weights and measures to sell less of his product for more money than it would normally fetch at the true market price.

c. Control or influence of the market can be seen through taxation, when a king might take money or crops from a people for his own use.

d. The point of all this is that in each of these instances, someone is exerting influence to try to control some aspect of the market for his own purposes and benefit. Such economic control and influence has happened throughout history in every country, and continues up to this day. There are endless markets everywhere; and someone is always trying to control them to a greater or lesser degree. As a result, every economic system that exists in the world today can be understood in regard to how much control it is trying to exert over markets.

B. What does this look like in real life? To help our thinking, let's imagine a long line:

i. At one end would be a true free market economic system where laws are simply put in place to safeguard private property and free exchange.

a. There has never been a completely free market economy in practice. Because of sin, no government will ever let an economic system be completely free; there's always someone who is trying to exert some influence, no matter how laws are set up to protect markets and make them free.

b. During the nineteenth century in England and America, however, there was more economic freedom than any other country at any other time in the history of the world. In both places, men inside the government actively worked to keep government intervention in the market at minimal levels.

ii. As we progress in the other direction, it means that *governments are intervening* more and more in the way their markets work.

   a. For instance, a government might put price controls on particular products. Or it might have increasing taxation. Or it might regulate what can be produced and what can't be produced. Or it might establish protective tariffs on imports.

   b. In all these instances, the government is intervening in the market; or, as one economist has said, the government is *hampering* the market. In these economies, the government is not doing away with the market, but is trying to control some aspect of it for specific reasons, normally its own benefit or the benefit of those controlling the government at that particular time.

   c. What are some examples of growing interventionism? The US economy from the 1860's forward, starting with the Civil War and showing increasing intervention up to the present day. You'll find all European countries and other countries of the world somewhere in this region. For instance, modern Hong Kong and New Zealand are less interventionist compared to countries like modern France or Germany. When looked at together, however, they would all be considered *interventionist* economies since they have not done away with free markets, but are hampering or restricting their movements to a greater or lesser degree.

iii. At the far end of the spectrum are the economic systems that seek to control markets entirely to the point of removing them. These are known as *command and control* economies, since some small group of individuals tries to control their entire economy through specific commands. They are also known as *socialist* economies since a small group of people are controlling the economy for what they say is the good of society (but usually ends up being for the good of that small group and its supporters).

   a. In these economies, private property and free exchange between people are banned or highly controlled, and the government tries to control and structure the entire economy.
   b. Although kings and leaders in the past often tried to control their economies to some degree, the first major economy to attempt complete socialist economic control was the Soviet Union in 1917, then China and North Korea in 1949, and others like Cuba, Vietnam, and the so-called Soviet-bloc countries.
   c. After the breakup of the Soviet Union in 1989, some of these countries have tried to

implement aspects of market economies, but the fact is, many are still heavily influenced by the State, and are far from being free market economies.

4. Economic Systems—the four basic questions.
   A. Economists have come up with a series of simple questions that are related to economic stewardship in a very basic way. These four questions have to be answered by every economy, although the answers differ significantly from system to system. The questions are:
      i. What will be produced?
      ii. Who will produce it?
      iii. How will it be produced?
      iv. For whom will it be produced?
   B. In terms of free market economies, the answer to each of the four questions is the same: every individual decides for himself, his family, and his business what will be produced, who will produce it, how it will be produced, and who it will be produced for.
      i. The key questions are answered differently by individuals who make up the free community of a free market. In other words, there are millions of different answers, and those answers change on a daily basis.
         a. The free market is a bee-hive of people trying to figure out better and better ways to answer these questions for themselves. After all, in a free market, everyone can do whatever he or she wants with their land, labor, and capital under the law.

ii. What does this mean for private property?
   a. The government has minimal to no control of private property through taxation or other means. It does not seek to build up public lands, but instead almost everything in the community is owned by individuals acting on their own behalf or as groups of individuals acting together (such as a for-profit business or a not-for-profit organization).
   b. This is a key aspect for Christian stewardship: it enables Christians to use their property to build up the Kingdom of God as they see fit. Those nations with the greatest protection of private property enable the most freedom to the growth of the church.

iii. As for vocation, individuals are free to choose their work based on their situation and abilities. This means that the division of labor is as complex and coordinated as those who make up the market want it to be.

iv. Concerning production and consumption, the market is driven by the free choices of consumers, and that which is produced is offered freely to all. Producers may make and sell what they want, so long as they can find a buyer.

v. Prices are based solely on the market forces of supply and demand. People are free to ask any price or pay any price.

vi. Trade is free. The only limits apply to things that are considered outside the moral bounds of God's law.

vii. In a free market, what is used for money is established by the market. Although we'll spend an entire lesson on money, here we're describing it simply as the most marketable commodity. The government does not step in and tell people what they have to use as money. In a truly free market, interest rates are set by the free interchange of the market instead of the government, thereby enabling people to save and invest based on real market indicators.

viii. Business is always privately held and entrepreneurs are the drivers of economic growth. In this economy, the government does not give special privileges or make special allowances for any particular business. Instead, the primary role of the government is to protect individual liberties and private property.

ix. To finish up our look at free market economies, they are sometimes referred to by other names like free enterprise, free trade, or *capitalist*. Let's talk a moment about capitalism:

   a. Historically, capitalism has been associated with private ownership of the means of production and use of capital within free markets. For generations, it was the term used to describe the economic system that developed in the West after feudalism.

   b. The problem today, however, is that different people define capitalism differently. When some people use the term they are actually referring to the free market; when others use it, they are referring to a system that politically favors capitalists. To avoid adding to this confusion, we have chosen to use the term 'free market' since it emphasizes liberty and choice within a market-based system.

C. If we jump to the far side of the spectrum, we arrive at *socialist* economies. A socialist, or command and control economy, believes these four questions can only be decided by a few central planners in the national government (or the State). Socialism seeks to control all the means of production through the so-called cooperation of the entire society. But history shows us that control always ends up in just a few hands.
   i. These central planners (or bureaucrats) tell individuals and businesses what to do in terms of the land, labor and capital used in production.
      a. In a socialist economy, the government will often present itself in a unique *collective* aspect as if all the people willingly joined together to act as the State. This collective idea of the many working together as one body is a conceptual cover for the fact that only a few individuals really control the lives of the majority, who have limited or no power within the State. Historically, all socialist economies work like this.
   ii. In a socialist economy, there is no true private property; rather everything is ultimately owned by the State and assigned to people for their use.

iii. Vocation is controlled by the State. There's no labor market; all jobs are determined by central planners.
iv. All production and consumption are determined by the State: economic goods are rationed out depending on what the State deems appropriate.
v. Prices are set by the State since there is no available market for supply and demand to determine prices.
vi. The money supply is determined by the State. Saving and investment are irrelevant—there's no market to determine interest rates, nor businesses to take risks on.
vii. Historically, there have been two distinct types of socialist economies: communist and nationalist.
    a. In *communism*, the State ultimately controls all property, and purposes the use of everything. This was the case in the Soviet Union and Soviet China, as well as the current case in North Korea and Cuba. Although the original communist thinkers believed it possible to create a society without ownership, even Lenin could not do it and so had to introduce some aspects of private ownership and markets back into their system with the so-called New Economic Policy in 1921. Nevertheless, the State at any time could step in and repossess anything in the country.
    b. In contrast, *national socialism* says individuals and businesses can own property, they just can't *control* or determine the ultimate

purpose of it. That was the case in Germany during WWI and again when the National Socialists were voted into power in 1933. This system means the state functionally controls everything.

viii. There are also two routes to socialism: revolutionary and evolutionary.

a. *Revolutionary* socialism can be seen in the Russian Revolution when Communists took over the government in 1917. Here socialism comes suddenly and in one dramatic action.

b. *Evolutionary* socialism can be seen in the process the Fabian society took in Britain starting in the 1880's. They worked slowly to implement socialist policies in the country, culminating in the 1940's socialist-leaning Labour government. Evolutionary socialism occurs over generations as more and more parts of the society are brought under national control or influence.

ix. Just like free markets have different names, socialist economies also have different names, such as totalitarianism, collectivism and social democracy. They also have been called by the names of some of their most famous proponents, such as Marxism and Leninism. Although differing in certain respects, they are all still socialism.

D. Next, we return to the middle of the spectrum and those economic systems known as *interventionist economies.*

i. In these economies, governments are intervening to a greater or lesser degree in the way their markets work. Depending on the country, some lean toward more freedom and others toward more control.

ii. What about our four key questions? Depending on the actual economy, they are normally answered by saying individuals have some economic latitude within specific economic constraints established by the government. And those constraints differ from country to country.

iii. Interventionist economies are always moving toward free markets or toward socialism depending on their current economic policies. The interventionist economy in its modern form is a market economy that is not really free, but is being hampered by individuals acting through the government.

  a. The argument usually made in favor of such an economy is that a free market must be regulated by the government in order to be most efficient, as well as to protect individuals. Yet, this goes directly against the idea that God created man to work most efficiently and effectively as a steward within free markets without any outside intervention.

  b. The 'government is more efficient' argument is really code for 'some individuals would like to direct the economy in ways that will help them out at the expense of other individuals' freedom and property.' Imagine someone saying, "it will be safer and better for you if I control your money, your property, and your business on your behalf." If it sounds crazy on an individual level, how much more so on a national level?

iv. Although we could use any number of interventionist economies as our example, we will talk about the modern United States, which is a good picture of a market economy that has a significant amount of government intervention.

v. Let's start with how interventionism approaches private property. In the United States, there is some respect for private property, yet ultimately the government controls how much property people can have, and what they do with it.

   a. This is the point of the current tax system: it takes private property from some groups (in the form of money) and gives it to other groups. If you think the government doesn't control from a quarter to a half of the private property you earn every year through trading your labor for money, just try not paying your taxes.

vi. Who controls land, labor and capital? Individuals control it within parameters set by the government.

vii. Can land be bought and sold without government taxation or regulation? No. That means government is intervening in the land market.

viii. Is there a minimum wage law? Yes. That means government is intervening in the labor market.

ix. Does the Federal Reserve control interest rates? Yes. That means the government (or in this case, a quasi-governmental institution) is intervening with the capital market.

x. Does the market set prices? In some instances it does, but in some the government may decide to step in with mandated price ceilings (someone cannot charge more than a certain price) or price floors (someone cannot charge less than a certain price).

xi. How about production and consumption? Again, partially free, but it is clear the government tries to encourage the production of certain things through monetary subsidies and penalizes the production of other things through additional taxes and fees.

xii. The modern United States is not a free market economy. Rather, it is an interventionist economy, where the government continually reaches in and hampers the market in some way or another.

    a. Such intervention happens in complex and sometimes quite subtle ways, but the fact is, our government levies significant taxes on individuals and businesses to redistribute that money among different sectors of society based on the decisions of central planners (in our case, unelected bureaucrats and elected officials).

b. From a Christian perspective, this is a serious problem. After all, if those central planners happen to be antithetical to Christianity, then they can take the money taxed from one group (such as Christians) and use it to support the actions of groups which work in direct support of Satan and his kingdom: Planned Parenthood is a case in point.

5. In closing, let's make one final connection. The nations that are known for their socialist systems are also known for their consistent persecution of Christians.
   A. They understand that there's a connection between economic liberty and religious liberty. When we give up economic liberty, we give up religious liberty.
   B. This means that pressure in the modern interventionist economies to move toward socialism doesn't just affect our pocketbooks, it also affects our ability to worship God.
   C. Those who do not want us to be stewards before God will seek to control our economic lives; we should instead strive for economic freedom and liberty since it ensures we will have the freedoms we need to worship God and build up His Kingdom.

MULTIPLE CHOICE

1. ________ is the foundation of a Christian economic philosophy.
   a. Biblical inerrancy
   b. Stewardship
   c. Financial accountability
   d. Private ownership of property

2. In an atheistic system, the State determines the purposes man will have with any ______.
   a. vocational endeavor
   b. land, labor or capital
   c. economic intentions
   d. financial system

3. In ______ economies, the government is not doing away with the market, but is trying to control some aspect of it for specific reasons, normally its own benefit or the benefit of those controlling the government at that particular time.
   a. interventionist
   b. socialist
   c. free market
   d. command and control

4. ______ occurs over generations as more and more parts of the society are brought under national control or influence.
   a. Progressive taxation
   b. Economic hampering
   c. Evolutionary socialism
   d. Privatization of property

5. Pressure in the modern interventionist economies to move toward socialism doesn't just affect our pocketbooks, it also affects our ______.
   a. return on investment
   b. economic indicators
   c. freedom to trade
   d. ability to worship God

SHORT ANSWER

1. Explain the "North Star" principle and apply it to some area of the modern economy.

2. Why is it unnecessary for the free market to be regulated by the government? What do such calls for regulation usually mean?

3. How does the interventionist economy of your country affect the way that you or the people that you know steward private property effectively?

DISCUSSION

1. Apply the "North Star" Principle to your particular vocation. How easy or difficult is it for you be a steward in what you do?
2. Why would a nation desire to implement interventionist (or even socialist policies) in their economic systems?
3. If you look around at society, what areas of intervention are pushing against the church and what it seeks to accomplish in the world? What can be done about it?
4. Explain some of the differences between free market, interventionist, and socialist systems in terms of: private property, vocation, taxation, money supply, and other relevant areas.

5. What do you know about the persecuted church around the world? How much of it is related to politics and economics?

FOR FURTHER STUDY

Basic Economics, 3rd Ed.—Carson & Cleveland—Chapters 18, 21
Foundations of Economics—Ritenour—Chapter 18
Economics: Principles and Policies—Rose—Chapter 8

Multiple choice answers: 1.d 2.b 3.a 4.c 5.d

8

Government Intervention: Basic Principles and Education

MESSAGE INTRODUCTION

Government intervention in an economy can significantly affect the ability of Christians to be faithful stewards. In this lesson, we will look at an example of government expansion from WWI Germany; at the basics of intervention; at a brief history of intervention in the US; and at the effects of intervention on education.

SCRIPTURE READING

Deuteronomy 6

LEARNING OBJECTIVES

1. To understand the nature and effects of government intervention on an economy.
2. To see the basic problems of intervention.
3. To recognize the impact of intervention on education and what that means for Christians.

QUOTATIONS

What are the sacred lies? The first and biggest lie is the notion that the institution of government is capable of successfully and adequately addressing all human problems. The truth is that such collectivism hampers human progress because it opens the door for many flagrant abuses of people and their property rights. It provides the greater means by which some people will invariably attempt to make their way in this world off the productive efforts of others.... The widespread belief that government can provide superior education, adequate retirement funds, and a whole host of other goods and services bears witness to the lie. Moreover, the common belief that people have that the government can successfully plan and manage the economy is additional evidence of the success of the lie.

—Paul Cleveland, *Unmasking the Sacred Lies*

LECTURE OUTLINE

1. Introduction to Government Intervention
   A. This is a true story that shows what happens when the government starts making economic decisions for its citizens beyond merely protecting life and private property.
   B. In Germany, during the First World War, there was massive inflation as a result of the hostilities. Prices began to rise, including the price of milk. The German people said the government needed to step in and set a maximum price for milk to enable more people to buy it. This maximum price was naturally lower than what milk was then costing on the free market.
   C. The government did this, passing a law that no one could charge more than so many marks for a liter

of milk. Many people thought they had solved the problem. But not long after passing this law, what happened? Instead of everyone being able to afford milk, there was an unexpected shortage of milk!

D. Why is it that the intended effect of passing this law—providing more milk for people at a lower price—actually had the unintended effect of creating a shortage? And what does this begin to tell us about the *unintended consequences* of government intervention in the market? Here's what happened to cause the shortage:
   i. First, the lowered price of milk increased the demand for it. Remember the laws of supply and demand: the artificially low price set by the government simply enabled more people to buy—so they did.
   ii. As a result, dairy farmers were forced to take losses for selling milk, something they could not sustain for long without losing money and eventually going bankrupt. What did they do?
   iii. Those farmers for whom it cost the most to sell milk—the marginal producers—stopped selling milk and instead started making cheese or butter. Some even sold their cows for meat since it was now more profitable to sell beef than to sell milk. This, of course, meant there was even *less* milk to be sold to even more people, resulting in a drastic shortage.
   iv. Although the government may have had a good intention by trying to control the price of milk, the result was far less milk for people than before the government started to intervene.

v. In light of the shortage, many people hurried to the shops to be there when the milk first arrived. Lines formed and could be seen around the cities. (These lines, by the way, always appear when the government tries to control the prices of certain commodities.)

E. What happened next? The government asked the dairy farmers why they were not making more milk. The farmers said their losses were too great because the cost of milk production was higher than the prices the government set.

F. The government's solution? Start controlling the price of cow fodder. But guess what? The same thing happened to cow fodder that happened to milk. By that point, it wasn't just milk the government was trying to control; they also started to control the prices on things like eggs, meat and other commodities—but with the exact same results. Nevertheless, instead of realizing that government price controls were the cause of the shortages, the government just kept moving up the production chain controlling the prices on more and more things. This constant push to control different aspects of the market economy eventually required them to control labor and wages, since that was also a key cost in production.

G. From an economic perspective, government intervention in the economy eventually moves toward socialism: the control of all prices, all production, all wages, all interest rates, and so on.

i. Although such things normally might take generations to happen, this happened within four years; the Germans actually created a system for it called The Hindenburg Plan. Everything was to be controlled by the government bureaucracy. Prices, wages, interest rates, everything.

ii. Yet, as the government was trying to fully implement the Hindenberg plan, Germany lost the war, the government was overthrown and the plan scrapped.

H. Before we leave this story, here are a few questions:

i. What if your vocation was a dairy farmer? What would this do to your business if you were forced to sell your milk below your production costs? Wouldn't this drive you out of business?

ii. Isn't it an example of the government deciding to take what was yours and ultimately give it to someone else? Specifically, the person who is now buying your milk at a below-market price? Isn't this really a subtle form of stealing?

iii. Of course, it shows that when the government steps in and tries to control aspects of the economy, even if it's with the best intentions, it immediately starts to affect an individual's ability to be a steward with what God has given him. And that's the primary problem with government intervention in the economy.

2. The Basics of Government Intervention

A. The government always has an economic role. It's necessary for a political system to establish an economic system. But what is the extent of that role? And what are its effects on man's ability to be a steward?

B. In a free market, the role of the government is simply to protect life and private property. The government does this by force; as we said before, the government has the power of the sword to accomplish its goals.
   i. When, however, people begin to think the government should go beyond its basic function of protection and begin to use its sword to influence economic decisions in order to try to address certain social needs—such as helping the poor or educating society—then it is taking authority from the realms decreed by God to address those needs (i.e., the family and the church).
   ii. Because of the way God has set up economic laws and relationships, when a government oversteps its bounds and tries to influence the economy, it always leads to failure. The unintended consequences of government intervention ultimately and consistently make a problem worse. Why is this?
   iii. It's because God did not establish government to do many of the things modern governments try to do. The economic laws of the universe will ultimately frustrate a society that tries to use its government in ways not designed by God. It's the necessary fate of government intervention in the economy. History bears witness to this time and again.
C. We defined interventionism as the government interfering with the market in order to try to influence it toward certain ends or goals. Interventionism means

that the government is not outlawing markets, but doing things to change the free outcomes of various markets inside the country.

i. Not all government intervention is the same: some countries are highly interventionist and some are only moderately so. Nevertheless, all the people who control modern governments are convinced they can do some good by controlling their economies.

D. Government can intervene in the economy in a number of ways. It can tax. It can spend through subsidies and redistribution. It can control prices. It can set up tariffs that protect certain industries from imports.

i. However, it's important to remember that a government cannot produce anything; it can only restrict, consume, and redirect. This is because it's defined by the sword, not the plow.

ii. God has made production the basis of economic growth. If a government cannot produce anything but only restrict, then this means that government intervention in the economy will ultimately restrict long-term economic growth. The greater the intervention, the greater the restriction. The greater the restriction, the faster a nation heads toward poverty. This is the long term economic curse of government overstepping its bounds.

E. Throughout the world, the history of government attempts at taking over the role of entrepreneurs continues to be a grand failure. Why can the government not run a business effectively?

i. The government does not have any real motivation or requirement to be profitable: the bureaucrats who control the money don't have any personal financial ownership in what they are doing. Simply put, the profit principle is impossible within government.
ii. This lack of financial accountability means government planners don't have the ability to make accurate economic calculations as to where or how to use their means of production.
iii. After all, what happens if they make bad decisions and lose money? They can't go out of business since they are part of the government. Instead, they run a deficit and taxpayers foot the bill. This situation is nothing new with government-run businesses.

F. Then why would anyone want government involved in the economy?
   i. One argument is that the free market does not work well on its own and requires someone to control the outcome. Someone must be planning, otherwise, things get out of control and end up badly for everyone.
      a. This is one of the great myths perpetrated on modern men. After all, from what we've already seen, God has made individual men owning private property and trading together in markets as the most efficient way for man to organize himself economically.
      b. We have seen that markets can be miniscule or unfathomably complex, and still work

incredibly well in allowing individuals to serve other individuals by meeting their needs as producers and consumers. There is nothing automatic about markets that can somehow get out of control; so long as a man's life, agreements and private property are being protected for him to produce according to his vocation and imagination, then the freedom to trade as he pleases will ensure that a society grows in wealth.

ii. Instead, the real reason for government intervention is always social and/or economic control; someone or some group is trying to control the economy for their own economic or social ends. Someone is trying to plan society in a particular way and harness economic policy to accomplish their objectives, often regardless of the long term economic consequences.

   a. The choice, therefore, is not between planning or not planning; rather the choice is between allowing individuals the freedom to plan their own lives versus granting power to the government to plan their lives for them.

   b. If some individual or some group is urging the government to overturn a natural market outcome, this really means that that individual or group wants armed men to implement their economic ends at the expense of other men freely coming together to trade under the law. There is a constant struggle between freedom and government control in every modern nation.

3. What does it really look like for the government to intervene in the market? What are the economic results? And why should Christians be concerned about it? In other words, what does interventionism mean for stewardship?
   A. Interventionism is a restriction of the free market that confuses or prevents real economic calculation. The government can take a number of actions to restrict the free market, but the long term results are consistently the same: limiting freedom and thereby limiting man's ability to be a steward. Those limits may seem minor in some instances and major in others. Either way, government intervention means that someone is stopping someone else from exercising his or her God-given freedoms. Restriction and control are not production; they are attempts at *influencing* production.
   B. Because interventionism prevents economic calculation, it ultimately cannot achieve the aims its implementers desire. What are the three main problems that ultimately face governments that attempt to control more and more aspects of their economies?
      i. Intervention aims at seizing the surplus from one and giving it to another, thereby undermining God's laws concerning private property. The 8th commandment applies to governments as much as to people. Taking from one by threatened force (such as jail) and giving to another is stealing.
         a. In the West, this form of stealing has been developed to a massive degree.
         b. In a free market, surplus is used by producers for producing new things that consumers want. In an interventionist economy, surplus is diverted to where those controlling the

economy desire, and inevitably away from the most consumer-oriented areas of production. Over time, because it is a violation both of moral and economic laws, it is doomed to failure. Once the surplus is used up, interventionism (and that society) must end.

ii. Initial intervention in the market always fails to achieve the ultimate ends sought, so more intervention has to be applied. This becomes a widening spiral of greater governmental control. Just look at the history of almost all governments in the West during the twentieth century and you will see how a small initial control always leads to greater and more invasive controls, thereby stripping more and more control away from the individual steward.

iii. As interventionism grows throughout a nation's economy, it slowly but inevitably pushes that nation toward socialism.

   a. Unlike communist socialism that starts violently, democratic or evolutionary socialism progresses from generation to generation and is the result of growing government intervention.

   b. Its initial failures lead to new economic controls and modes of seizing the surplus from one and giving it to another. This type of socialism is like the Hindenberg socialism of Germany in WWI; it has overtaken all the governments of Western Europe by now and has made much headway in the United States.

4. Over this and the two following lessons, we'll take a look at the United States to see what the struggle between free markets and government intervention looks like in detail, especially how it bears upon Christian stewardship.
   A. Remember: the United States has been one of the most important Christian nations in the history of the world. Individual believers and churches have contributed significantly toward the advancement of Christ's Kingdom.
   B. In many ways, Britain in the nineteenth century and the US in the twentieth century have been the great missionary-sending and world-evangelization-financing nations. This fact has not been lost on Satan, and one of the ways he has tried to control that influence is by confusing both nations' economic thinking.
   C. The histories of the US and Britain are therefore revealing as to how they have become more interventionist as they moved toward socialism over the past 150 years. Although we will be focusing on the US in this study, Britain was pushed far into the camp of socialism during the twentieth century with devastating effects on its national economy. (And, interestingly enough, paralleled by a dwindling population in the Christian church.)
   D. From one perspective, the US is just a few steps behind Britain. The twentieth-century movement in the US toward socialism has had a direct influence on Christians in significant and problematic ways.
   E. Since we'll be jumping around a bit in these lessons, here's a brief history of the US economy. This should help us put things in perspective and remind us that

what's happening today is a departure from our beginnings.

i. *Constitutional Republic: 1789–1860*—This was the great free market period of our nation that laid the foundations of our international rise to power.
   a. The people of this period generally followed Jefferson's view of government and economics, although there was always a desire from Hamilton and others for greater central economic control.
   b. The two great economic injustices during this time were slavery and protectionist tariffs. Although slavery is one of the great economic crimes committed against a people within the United States (abortion, actually, is the worst), it is important to remember that it was a common feature of world history up until the eighteenth century. Sinful thinking often takes many generations to overcome.

ii. *Civil War & Rise of Corporatism: 1860–1910*—Corporatism is the economic influence over government by business interests.
   1. The Whig-Republicans took over the Presidency and Congress in 1861 and immediately began passing bills supportive of Northern businesses—basically, the tariff against industrial imports from England. There were still many free market aspects to our nation, but the size and power of government began to grow under Lincoln and his successors.

2. The Civil War centralized many economic and political features of the nation. In fact, it is always during US wars that greater economic control is sought under the argument of necessity. After the war, however, those controls are not readily relinquished.

iii. *Progressive Era & WWI Centralization: 1910–1932*—Social reformers desired to pay for a variety of new social programs by means of the government coffers; forward-thinking politicians realized the voting blocs that could be influenced at the same time. This was the period when socialism began to be accepted within American academic and political circles. As one writer visiting Soviet Russia artfully said: "I've seen the future, and it works." (Unfortunately, he just didn't see far enough.)

a. Although initially unconstitutional, the 16th amendment established the income tax across the nation pitting the poor against the rich: at the time, it started at 1% and went to 7% highest tax rate (this provides us some perspective on how it has grown in 100 years).

b. The larger banks and the government worked together to create the Federal Reserve Banking System in 1913 to control the nation's money supply, among other useful things.

c. WWI introduced radically extensive war controls on the economy. Although the government of the 1920's retreated from much of this centralization, it did not retreat as far as it could have.

iv. *New Deal Socialism: 1932–1960*—Roosevelt's New Deal was the introduction of the majority of the socialist-based programs that are still with us today (in some form or another).
   a. These programs included: the Social Security Administration, the National Recovery Administration, the Works Progress Administration, and so on.
   b. WWII added many new economic controls that were considered necessary for fighting the war. Again, centralization of politics and economics is a hallmark of wartime.

v. *Interest Group Liberalism and Welfarism: 1960 to Present*—The welfare state introduced by FDR continued to expand under Truman, Eisenhower, Kennedy, Johnson, Nixon and forward to today.
   a. New programs like Medicare and Medicaid, although perhaps well-meaning, created a whole new series of welfare entitlements in the 1960s that have primarily grown and expanded since then.
   b. Special interest groups began to work the political spectrum through a refined corporatism with the goal of trying to transfer taxpayer dollars into their businesses by means of government contracts, subsidies, and other wealth transfers.

F. There has been a monumental growth in government spending throughout the twentieth century. The government has clearly overstepped its bounds and tried to control and influence more and more parts of the US economy. What are they trying to control?
   i. Just look at the President's 15 executive cabinet positions and you get a snapshot of the industries most tied to the government: Defense, Labor, Health, Agriculture, Commerce, Energy, Interior, Housing, Transportation, and so on.
   ii. One of the most influential areas of control received 15% of national, state and local budgets for 2010. As we look deeper into government intervention, let's begin with the most influential area that affects every other area.

5. *Education* may seem like a strange place to start talking about the impact of government intervention in the economy, but it's the best place for two important reasons:
   A. Education determines how a culture understands and engages the world, including the way it practices economics.
      i. If you want to influence a society socially and economically then control how and what it teaches its children. This is why the Bible makes parents the primary educational authority for children. A nation's ability to develop one generation after another of good, Biblical stewards is tied directly to how it educates them. If a culture doesn't really understand economics, it will be much easier to mislead economically.

   ii. Second, if you want to reduce the influence of Biblical Christianity on a people, then just control their education. Since such control would be difficult to obtain with consistency at a local level, it would be necessary to establish some kind of centralized government intervention over education, first at the state level, then at the federal level. This is exactly what happened in the US.

B. Education was one of the first areas to be taken over by men and women whose primary goal was to change the social order in the United States. As a result, US public education has been re-structured to reflect a socialist organization from top to bottom. Most people don't realize it, but the American public education system is the most socialistic institution in the country. Even its leaders recognize that:

   i. "It's time to admit that public education operates like a planned economy, a bureaucratic system in which everybody's role is spelled out in advance and there are few incentives for innovation and productivity. It's no surprise that our school system doesn't improve: It more resembles the communist economy than our own market economy."—Albert Shanker, *American Federation of Teachers (Wall Street Journal, October 2, 1989)*

C. Here are a few ways public education is socialist:

   i. It is centrally-controlled from the federal and state levels, not the parental level;

   ii. It is a monopoly that exists through compulsion—it has traditionally forced parents using the governmental sword to send their children to certain schools;

iii. It is completely funded by re-distribution of wealth (tax dollars);

iv. It is controlled by an entrenched bureaucracy that denies merit and competition;

v. It is completely atheistic in its approach to education, denying God and Christianity at all levels.

vi. For our purposes, we will look at US public education as a prime example of what happens when government intervenes in order to try to control social and economic outcomes.

D. American public education is socialist both in its structure and its content. Structure refers to the way the organization is put together; content refers to what is being taught.

i. In terms of structure, here's what happens when the government intervenes in the market for children's education.

a. Who are the true decision makers and consumers concerning children's education? Parents. God has made parents ultimately responsible for educating their children. In a free market, parents choose to educate their children however they wish in accordance with what they think is best: this might be at a local private school, this might be with a group of other children, this might be at a home. But none of these options are run by the state.

b. What happens when the state steps in and says it is responsible for a child's education and makes attendance to its schools 'free' and yet compulsory for all children? Education becomes a government-run monopoly that drives competition out of the market.
    1) Who is the competition? Parents and private schools. This is pretty much what happened in the US in the nineteenth and early twentieth centuries as public schools took over from parents and private education.
    2) Government intervention therefore confused and prevented real economic calculation by disconnecting consumers from control over the product.

c. As a result, educational quality declined over the twentieth century.
    1) Initial intervention in the market failed to achieve the ultimate ends the government sought, so more intervention had to be applied. This is because education was removed from its basic consumer: parents. Business thinking was removed from the situation and so there was no grounding in what was important or unimportant to consumers.
    2) Rather, central planners and bureaucrats decided what the schools should be teaching and how they should use the money provided by the government (or actually provided by parents through taxation, but no longer in the control of parents).

d. Money was taken from some taxpayers and given to others, thereby undermining God's laws concerning private property.
   1) It is now accepted that this is the "right" thing to do in terms of education. But any sector that is propped up by government money means that it has lost touch with the market and doesn't know what to do with the money it gets.
   2) Stealing implies there is no production involved, so the taker does not have the same sense of responsibility as the rightful owner. In fact, this is the curse of government dollars: without market feedback and the profit motive, those dollars will not be productive. Therefore things are spent haphazardly without any heed for results, and more and more taxpayer money is needed. (Sound familiar?)
e. But the delusion continues. Those who are convinced that government intervention must work just say that more money is necessary with better organization to solve the problem.
   1) This leads to greater central planning at higher cost in the hopes of trying to make things more efficient. Yet, ultimately, this has the reverse effect: greater loss of money with greater inefficiency. Just take a look at the hundreds of millions of dollars wasted annually on educational

administrators in the educational system from federal to local levels.

2) After all, without market feedback, those planners are absolutely disconnected from what is best educationally. They cannot do any kind of economic calculation.

ii. This is where we begin to move into content: because there is no responsibility to consumers concerning what they want to be taught, there is no real economic calculation in terms of cost.

a. In other words, a public school (unlike a private school) does not have to say "if I teach this, I'll lose students."

b. Hence, central planners can teach whatever they want without recourse to parents. Not only is this content the wrong content to be teaching (since it's based neither on market needs nor parental desires), the entire structure leads naturally to enormous waste and inefficiency.

iii. What is perhaps more shocking about education is that the economic consequences were irrelevant to those who formed this system: they just wanted control of the children and control of the content, with the assurance that parents would have no say in what was being taught.

a. This brings us back to the real purpose of government intervention: it's always social and/or economic control. Someone or some group is trying to control the economy for their own economic or social ends. In this case, the result has been the dumbing down and de-

Christianization of the entire nation over the process of 150 years. This has had grave effects spiritually, politically, and economically.

b. What are the obvious results of this kind of socialist educational structure? John Gatto spent 30 years in various New York City public classrooms and was the 1991 New York State Teacher of the Year. He says these are the seven lessons actually taught in public schools:
   1) Confusion
   2) Class Position
   3) Indifference
   4) Emotional Dependency
   5) Intellectual Dependency
   6) Provisional Self-Esteem
   7) No One Can Hide from Authority
c. Why are these the results? Because our government schools have this as its basic worldview:
   1) Christianity has nothing to do with any aspect of truth (the reason it is forbidden from all public school classrooms) and therefore there is no ultimate truth;
   2) Parents are not the source of wisdom or knowledge, some expert authority is (like a teacher);
   3) The government is responsible for your well-being, and your job is to submit to it (as you do for 12 years in school);
   4) Nothing is really connected to anything else (think about the randomness of

classes and courses), so therefore you can't link up the dots that you're really being controlled by other forces.

d. This may seem exceptional to many, but how else could a nation of Christians who were interested in stewardship, self-reliance, and productive work become a nation of anti-Christians who are interested in entertainment, dependence, and economic entitlement?
e. All the other interventionist economic policies we will look at in the coming lessons could never have happened unless the government had not first gotten involved in controlling education.

6. This is why God makes parents responsible for their children's education: it is a hedge against other people taking it over and changing the way they think.
   A. State-run, compulsory education is necessary to ensure that children think the way the individuals controlling the state want them to think and work in terms of economics. If they don't understand their responsibility economically to God, then they will naturally be much less effective in building up His Kingdom, and might even be co-opted in building up Satan's kingdom.
   B. A free educational system must have as its foundation God's law. It begins with parents controlling education that's not linked to the state.
      i. Moses says: *"And these words that I command you today shall be on your heart. You shall teach*

them diligently to your children, and shall talk of them when you sit in your house, and when you walk by the way, and when you lie down, and when you rise... So you shall keep the commandments of the Lord your God by walking in his ways and by fearing him..." (Deut. 6:6–7).

ii. *For the Lord your God is bringing you into a good land, a land of brooks of water, of fountains and springs, flowing out in the valleys and hills, a land of wheat and barley, of vines and fig trees and pomegranates, a land of olive trees and honey, a land in which you will eat bread without scarcity, in which you will lack nothing, a land whose stones are iron, and out of whose hills you can dig copper. And you shall eat and be full, and you shall bless the Lord your God for the good land he has given you*" (Deut. 8:7–10).

C. It is not the state but parents that have the ultimate responsibility for a child's education. God's economic blessings given to a nation are directly related to knowing and following His commands, something that begins with education. From an economic perspective, education is the basis of building an economy that enjoys both great freedom and great wealth.

MULTIPLE CHOICE

1. In a ________, the role of the government is simply to protect life and private property.
   a. socialist economy
   b. interventionist economy
   c. free market
   d. command and control

2. Because interventionism prevents ______, it ultimately cannot achieve the aims its implementers desire.
   a. economic calculation
   b. financial forecasting
   c. monetary inflation
   d. social organization

3. Initial intervention in the market always fails to achieve the ultimate ends sought, so more ______ has to be applied.
   a. economic freedom
   b. intervention
   c. price control
   d. welfare

4. As interventionism grows throughout a nation's economy, it slowly but inevitably pushes that nation toward ______.
   a. prosperity
   b. socialism
   c. nationalism
   d. progressivism

5. ______ determines how a culture understands and engages the world, including the way it practices economics.
   a. Philosophy
   b. Education
   c. Monetarism
   d. Interventionism

SHORT ANSWER

1. RC says 'the choice is not between planning and no planning, but between allowing individuals the freedom to plan their own lives versus granting power to the

government to plan their lives for them.' What are the implications on either side for Biblical stewardship?

2. Why is the impossibility of economic calculation such a problem for an interventionist economic system?

3. Why is education such an important part of an interventionist economy?

DISCUSSION

1. If government intervention confuses economic calculation within a market, talk about some areas you've seen this happen in the US through the use of government money in various industries.
2. Do you think the US has moved in the direction of socialism over the past 100 years? Why or why not? Name some specific examples one way or the other.
3. We've said some strong things about public education. What do you think about the current state of education in the US, and why do you think it's in that condition?

FOR FURTHER STUDY

Prosperity and Poverty—Beisner—Chapters 12–13
Unmasking the Sacred Lies—Cleveland—Chapter 6
Dumbing Us Down—Gatto—Chapter 1

Multiple choice answers: 1.c 2.a 3.b 4.b 5.b

9

Two Mysteries of Monetary Policy: Inflation and Depressions

MESSAGE INTRODUCTION

The fact that government and banking-system inflation leads to recessions/depressions has serious consequences for stewardship. In this lesson, we'll look at money; at interest rates; at the Federal Reserve Bank; at inflation; at the boom/bust cycle; and at the Great Depression.

SCRIPTURE READING

Deuteronomy 25:13–16
Genesis 47:15

LEARNING OBJECTIVES

1. To understand the impact inflation has on a nation's economy.
2. To see how the boom/bust cycle works.
3. To recognize the role the Federal Reserve Banking System plays in controlling and influencing the US economy.

QUOTATIONS

> *Our understanding and use of money, as individuals and whole societies, have a profound effect on the quality of our stewardship. A faulty money system can cause people to misjudge the value of their money and, hence, their ability to afford goods and services.... In short, a faulty monetary system can cause us to waste resources—resources over which God has made us stewards and for the use of which He will hold us accountable.*
>
> —E. Calvin Beisner, *Prosperity and Poverty*

LECTURE OUTLINE

1. Introduction to the Two Mysteries
   A. Mystery #1: What happened to the value of the dollar?
      i. If you talk to your grandparents about money, they'll likely remember that when they were growing up, prices were a lot lower than they are today.
      ii. Since things cost more now than they used to, money has lost a lot of its *purchasing power*. Money simply isn't as valuable as it used to be. If it once cost a nickel to get candy bar, but it costs a dollar today, that's a significant loss in value. Where did the value of our money go?
      iii. As of 2012, the US dollar had lost about 97% of its value compared to 100 years ago. Someone actually took that value—but who? And why? Is this not a form of stealing? A nation-wide breaking of the 8th commandment? This is the first mystery.

B. Mystery #2: What caused the Great Depression and why was it so great?
   i. Most people have a sense of how bad the Great Depression was, how long it lasted, and what a burden it was on the nation. There hasn't been anything exactly like it since then, although there have been many severe recessions (and some would even say our current economic recession is really a depression).
      a. Conventional wisdom says the government saved us from the Great Depression. Is that true?
      b. What if it was really government intervention that got us into the depression, and then government intervention that made it last so long? What if some groups want us to think that it's the free market that causes recessions/depressions, when it's really the result of other groups trying to control the economy?
      c. If that is true, this would be a violation of the 9th commandment on a national scale. This is the second mystery.

C. In this lesson, we will look at *money*, one of the most important parts of a nation's economic system. We'll also look at how government intervention has put our monetary system in a very dangerous and dishonest place.

D. What is the impact of money on the church? For the moment, let's apply our North Star principle: how does the devaluation of money or a national recession affect man's ability to be a God-obeying steward of creation?

i. If money is devalued over time, then Christians are less able to use that money to be effective stewards. Look at it this way: if someone is taking money out of your bank account every year, doesn't that give you less to apply toward your vocation and kingdom-building endeavors?
ii. Furthermore, during a recession or depression, Christians go bankrupt just like non-Christians; church revenues go down because of less tithing; countless ministries struggle to raise money and some ministries and churches must shut their doors; ministers are laid off; missionaries struggle with support; and enormous numbers of Christians lose their wealth and struggle just to make ends meet. The division of labor begins to break down, divorce rates go up, birth rates go down, and people just basically struggle.
iii. What a government does with money, therefore, has an enormous impact on the ability of Christians to be good stewards and to pursue their vocations.

2. In Lesson 4, we looked briefly at money, but we're now going deeper.
   A. Money is a means of exchange for an economy. Throughout history, we've seen commodities like tobacco, salt, shells, copper, silver, gold and paper be used as money in exchange and trade. Because of that, it is also:
      i. *A unit of account*. Money needs to provide accurate and precise valuations from one person to another in a society. If three different things

each cost one silver coin, then everyone knows the market value for those items.

ii. *A store of value.* Money must also maintain its value over time. A merchant who trades his goods for coins in January wants those coins to be worth the same amount in June. A commodity must hold its value over time for it to be good money.

B. There are also five aspects that make a commodity useful as money.

i. Divisibility—you can divide it up easily;
ii. Portability—you can carry it around with you;
iii. Durability—it doesn't go away over time;
iv. Recognizability—everyone knows what it is by sight;
v. Scarcity—there's not that much of it around.

C. Historically, money was not originally determined by the government, but by the market. In most societies, however, once something is decided on as money by the market, the government then takes over control of it.

i. Gold, silver and copper have most widely been used for money. God created these metals with the characteristics that made them more likely to be used as money.

ii. Why is gold still valuable and the best money?

a. If you compare it to all the qualifications listed above, it is the perfect fit.

b. Furthermore, many people would say that God made man to value gold from the beginning. Interestingly enough, it is the first precious metal to be mentioned in the Bible: *A river flowed out of Eden to water the garden, and there it divided and became four rivers. The name of the first is the Pishon. It is the one that flowed around the whole land of Havilah, where there is gold. And the gold of that land is good; bdellium and onyx stone are there* (Gen. 2:10–12).

iii. What gets used for money today?

   a. Primarily paper and digits. Do paper and digits have the 5 aspects of money? Not all. It's easy to print more paper and make more zeros and ones; digits and paper are not naturally scarce.

   b. How do you make paper and digits used as money scarce? One way is to link paper and digits to a real commodity, for instance, gold or silver. Another way is to limit the amount that is created (but this has never actually worked historically: it's too easy to print more paper and generate more digits.)

D. Money is the lifeblood of a market economy: it may seem like a minor thing, but it ensures that all the endless back-and-forth transfers in an economy move smoothly. Without it, an economy will not work. If it is abused, it can actually stop working and destroy the economy of an entire nation. (Just think of Germany in 1923, or Zimbabwe more recently.)

E. The Bible talks a lot about money, especially being honest with it:

   i. *You shall do no wrong in judgment, in measures of length or weight or quantity. You shall have just balances, just weights, a just ephah, and a just hin...* (Lev. 19:35, 36).

ii. *Unequal weights and unequal measures are both alike an abomination to the Lord* (Prov. 20:10).
iii. In these cases, honesty in measuring out whatever is used as money is very important in God's eyes. Why? Units of money are linked to its value; if one is dishonest about the units one is using (that is, saying it's more when it's really less), one is effectively taking value from someone else: in other words, stealing.
iv. Since God created man to use money, He understood its importance. But He also understood that if man loved money and cared more about it than God, it would become an idol.
    a. Paul tells us it's *the love* of money that's the source of all kinds of evil, not money itself. This is a very important distinction. *For the love of money is a root of all kinds of evils. It is through this craving that some have wandered away from the faith and pierced themselves with many pangs* (1 Tim. 6:10).
    b. Money is not bad in itself—as we said before, some of God's favorite people in the Bible were wealthy with gold and silver. God gives us many warnings about it, but primarily because it's so powerful and influential because of what it is.

3. Clues to the First Mystery—Who Controls Money?
    A. Banks are the backbone of every modern economic system. Banks control a society's money by storing and lending it (among other things).

i. When banks lend money, they charge an *interest rate*. An interest rate is simply the amount of additional money someone will pay to borrow a particular amount of money for a particular amount of time. For instance, if someone agrees to borrow $100 at a 6% interest rate over a one year period, he would owe the lender $106 at the end of the year. Another way of saying it would be that the interest rate is the price of present money in exchange for future money. Assuming everything is paid back in a year, someone will pay an additional $6 in the future to have $100 now.
   a. In a free market, interest rates fluctuate on the basis of supply and demand. If more people want to borrow a fixed supply of present money for future money, then interest rates will go up. If fewer people want that same supply, then interest rates will go down.

ii. Why are interest rates important? In a free market, <u>interest rates coordinate production and business decisions over time.</u> If interest rates are higher, people will make certain decisions about what to produce or not to produce; and if interest rates are lower, people will make different decisions.

iii. For example, suppose you're a home builder and you get out your pencil and crunch your numbers and you decide you can sell a house for 10% more than it costs you to build it.
   a. Let's say the bank is willing to loan money to you at a 4% interest rate. You likely want to

borrow a good amount of money and build a lot of houses because each house represents 6% profit for you.

b. But if interest rates are higher and it costs you 12% to borrow the money to build the houses, you won't build any houses. It's a loss this way. And, of course, if interest rates go even higher, you'll likely want to become a fireman.

iv. This is not an isolated example. All sorts of decisions based squarely on current interest rates happen every day across our economy affecting every possible industry.

B. Governments have also been a major influence in modern economic systems. Both banks and governments have a very keen desire to control money. Historically, both have sought to manipulate financial markets for their own purposes. When banks and governments come together to control the money supply, they create a *central bank*.

i. When the United States was founded, one of the most divisive issues was the question as to whether we should or should not establish a central bank.

a. Thomas Jefferson and James Madison fought strongly against such a bank, saying a central bank was unconstitutional. They believed the centralization of banking would be dangerous to a sound monetary system and to local banks.

b. Alexander Hamilton was the primary supporter, arguing a central bank was necessary for the financial growth of the nation in terms of credit and currency.

ii. After a long fight, the First Bank (and later the Second Bank) of the United States were created. But they ended up being as controversial in practice as they were in formation, so, in 1836, Andrew Jackson let the charter to the Second Bank expire.

iii. It was not until 1913 that the United States government again established a central bank when it founded the Federal Reserve Banking System (or the Fed, for short).

1. The stated goal of the Federal Reserve Act was to control the nation's monetary policy and influence employment, prices, and interest rates.
2. But who was behind it? A handful of big Wall Street banks and the United States government. Together they set up a partly governmental/partly private agency that has ultimate control over the nation's money supply.

4. More Clues to the First Mystery—Inflation after World War I

A. Right after the Federal Reserve was created, World War I broke out in Europe. Even though the US was not militarily involved at first, it was financially involved. WWI, like every other war, was very expensive. The government began to pour more and more money into helping finance the allies' military endeavors.

B. Where did the money come from? To finance a war, a government can borrow money, it can tax its populace, or, if it has a central bank, it can create new money. In other words, it can inflate the money supply. This last option is known as *inflation*.
   i. Inflation is popularly considered an increase in prices, but that's not the complete story. Inflation is really an increase in the money supply which eventually leads to an increase in prices.
   ii. In the United States, it is the Federal Reserve working in conjunction with other banks that inflate the US money supply.

C. During WWI, the United States was on a gold standard. This meant that $1 dollar was valued at 1/20 an ounce of gold (or $20 = 1 ounce). In 1916, if you had $20, you could go to a bank and redeem it for a one ounce gold coin.

D. Between 1916 and 1920, the supply of money in the United States went from $20 billion dollars to $35 billion dollars. That's a 70% increase in just five years. Did that mean 750 million ounces of gold were introduced into the economy? No. It meant the government started printing more paper and banks started adjusting the digits on journals. So what happened?
   i. The laws of supply and demand tell us that the prices of goods and services will rise when the money supply rises. This is because there are lots more dollars chasing the same amount of goods and services in the economy. Prices will rise to meet the money supply.
   ii. That's exactly what happened during and after WWI. Starting in 1916 and going all the way to

1920, the US saw year-after-year of double-digit inflation. If it is all added up, there was 85% inflation during that short time period.

E. For example, if you bought a gallon of milk in 1916, you might have expected to pay $.31. Fast forward just a few years to 1920. If you want to buy that same gallon of milk, it would cost $.57.
   i. But wait: money is supposed to be a store of value. In just four years, the dollar lost a lot of its purchasing power and value. To give it a contemporary perspective, a gallon of milk in 2008 would cost $4.00 but that same gallon of milk in 2012 would cost $7.40. Ouch.
   ii. Yet this value had to go somewhere—it didn't just disappear. Where did it go? The US government and banks took $.26 out of everyone's dollars in order to finance the war. <u>Inflation is a hidden tax.</u>
   iii. Yet how is the value taken? When the new money is printed, those who have access to it and spend it first get to use it at the current market prices. But as the new money is spent in the market, prices start to rise. Those who held onto their money and didn't spend it at the lower prices are the ones who ultimately have to pay the higher prices—all of which are a result of the increase in money supply in the first place!
   iv. Inflation rewards those who use the new money first and penalizes those who save their money.

F. Unfortunately, inflation didn't stop in 1920. Since 1914, every dollar in the United States has lost 97% of its value. In other words, what cost $30 in 1914 now costs $1000. But that $970 of value didn't just disappear—the government and the banking system essentially took it from everyone who owned dollars during that period.

i. Since, by law, the Federal Reserve is responsible for the nation's money supply, it is ultimately responsible for the dollar's loss in value.
ii. Where does it all stop? What is the end result? When the government and banks continue to devalue our currency, eventually people lose trust in their own money. When that happens, a whole system collapses.
iii. It has happened before in history: in Germany, as a result of WWI and the reparations leveled against them, they began to inflate their money supply. This inflation turned suddenly into hyperinflation (an unstoppable rise in prices) in 1922 and 1923. As a result, Germany's entire economy ground to a halt and they had to create a new currency. Eventually, this economic disorder led them to appoint a new leader who promised stability and economic growth through national socialism: Adolf Hitler.

G. Is there any plumb line that shows us how much our money has been devalued? Not surprisingly, gold serves that purpose.
    i. In 1914, gold was selling at approximately $20 an ounce. This amount was the gold standard that had been used in the United States since its founding.
    ii. As of 2011, the price of gold hit $1500 per ounce and has not dropped below it as of mid-2012.

iii. What this proves about intervention in the case of the dollar is that:
    a. It confuses and destroys economic calculation since interest rates and money supply are not market driven.
    b. It destroys long term individual savings;
    c. And it disrupts long term business decisions since dollars are not as effective as a store of value.

H. What are the ultimate results of inflation?
  i. It's stealing. When the government and banks inflate the money supply, they're silently taking the wealth from savings that is the stored value in the money of the people. Inflation takes that value and gives it to the government, to the banking industry, and to other close connections.
  ii. Second, while government may try to slow the inflation, their needs and desires are growing rapidly. And so the process actually begins to feed upon itself, where the government inflates more and more to meet its obligations while it devalues the money more and more at the same time.
  iii. Finally, inflation inevitably pushes us closer and closer to socialism. As prices rise, people turn to the government to stop them. When the government intervenes in the market to a greater degree, it only causes more problems which the people then demand the government to fix.
  iv. Here's how John Maynard Keynes says it works. Although ultimately a poor friend of

free markets, Keynes was one of the economists who predicted the problems that would happen in Germany after WWI. He explained: "Lenin is said to have declared that the best way to destroy the capitalist system was to debauch the currency. By a continuing process of inflation, governments can confiscate secretly and unobserved an important part of the wealth of their citizens. By this method, they not only confiscate but they confiscate arbitrarily, and while the process impoverishes many, it actually enriches some. As inflation proceeds and the real value of the currency fluctuates wildly from month to month, all permanent relations between debtors and creditors (which forms the ultimate foundation of capitalism) becomes so utterly disordered as to be almost meaningless. And the process of wealth-getting degenerates into a gamble and a lottery. Lenin was certainly right. There's no subtler, no surer means of overturning the existing basis of the society than to debauch their currency. The process engages all the hidden forces of economic law on the side of destruction, and does it in a manner which not one man in a million is able to diagnose." (John Maynard Keynes, *The Economic Consequences of the Peace*)

5. Clues to the Second Mystery: What caused the Depression?
   A. Unfortunately, devaluing the currency and transferring wealth from one group to another is not the only

problem with an inflationary monetary policy. An inflationary monetary policy ends up creating a boom/bust cycle in an economy.

i. Booms leading to busts leading to recessions (and even depressions in some cases) are the inevitable result of consistent inflation in an economic system.
ii. Understanding this relationship helps explain the cause of the Great Depression as well as all the recessions up to the present day.

B. If we return to the time right after WWI, the inflation of the money supply continues at double digits, year after year, when suddenly in late 1920 the economy goes into a tailspin and inflation suddenly stops.

i. Although something specific happened to trigger it, it was like someone bumping into a house of cards: the economy was vulnerable in any number of places because it wasn't built on real wealth.
ii. As a result, the inflation of the war years and immediately after led to the lesser-known Depression of 1920–21. In other words, significant intervention by a central bank pursuing an inflationary monetary policy is the root cause of depressions and recessions.

C. Now this isn't what is normally taught. Instead, we regularly hear the criticism that recessions/depressions are just an aspect of the free market that inevitably brings booms and busts, and that therefore the free market needs outside regulation.

i. Remember, though: whenever you hear that phrase "the free market needs regulation" you should start asking the question: who wants to control the free market? In this case, our partners in monetary policy: the government and the banks working together through the Federal Reserve.

ii. When the Fed creates money (or buys assets, as it is technically called), it first goes to a handful of big banks that have a unique relationship with it.

   a. These banks have the ability to inflate what they get from the Fed through something called a *money multiplier*. That is, they are allowed to create more new money themselves in the form of bank checks (among other options) and loan that out. They can do this up to 8 to 10x what they have on reserve at the Fed.

   b. This means banks regularly lend out much more money than they have on deposit in their bank. Is this an example of legal counterfeiting? Yes. Is it dishonest? Ultimately, yes—even if their customers sort of know they are doing it. What most people don't really understand is that this is part of the inflation of the money supply that is silently taking value from them over the long run.

D. For perspective, let's turn the tables: if you try to use more money than you have in your bank account, it's called overdrawing your account; and we all know that banks are not very lenient to those who overdraw their accounts.

   i. But what if banks didn't care? What if you could spend 10x more money than you actually had in your account? What if, in fact, *everyone* could do this? Wouldn't that inflate the money supply by an extraordinary amount?
   ii. It would inflate it, but it wouldn't be based on anything real, like a paycheck for work done or profits from a business. It would just be a fabrication.

E. But that's what all these banks are doing: overdrawing their account by multiplying the new money they get from the Federal Reserve as well as their own current holdings and loaning it out. They, of course, can then charge interest on all those loans making many times more than they could if they only loaned out what they had on hand. This creates a significant increase in the money supply and a drop in interest rates. The result?
   i. Low interest rates send a very strong message to producers and businesses: Produce! Create! Borrow! Invest!
   ii. But these interest rates influenced by the Fed are usually much lower than rates set freely by the market. As a result, the low interest rate fools all these entrepreneurs and business owners into making bad investment decisions simultaneously.
      a. But boy are those initial times great! This is why it's called a *boom*. Everything seems to be growing in every direction, people are making lots of money, unemployment is at record lows, and the economy is going gangbusters.

   b. This happened in the mid-1920's when the Federal Reserve again started lowering interest rates and increasing the money supply. We know this period as the Roaring 20's. And during that time, much of the newly created inflationary money went into the stock market driving up the prices of stock and creating what is known as a 'bubble.'

F. Yet since this new money wasn't based on anything real (like savings), there wasn't a long-term consumer ability to purchase or use all these new things that were being created. The buildings, the ships, the houses, the cars, etc., etc.
   i. Eventually, people started to realize that certain areas in the economy were overvalued. When people started realizing they had made mistakes, at first a few started to sell, then more, then suddenly *en masse* many in the market changed their behavior. Instead of buying, they sold. And when that happened, prices start to fall leading more people to sell.

G. This is what happened in October of 1929. There was a mass decision that stock prices had gone too high and everything came tumbling down.
   i. So, to be truly accurate, it wasn't the stock market crash that caused the depression of the 1930's: it was the inflationary money policy of the mid to late 1920's that found its way into the stock market, blew it up like a bubble, then popped in October 1929. This is the *bust* in the boom/bust cycle.

ii. Yet the entire economy was set for failure because so many entrepreneurs and investors had made bad decisions across all sorts of industries.

iii. What misled all these hundreds of thousands of people simultaneously to all make the same bad decisions across all the industries? An inflationary money supply and unreasonably low interest rates.

6. Stewardship and Inflation
   A. Let's bring back our North Star principle. The dishonest practices of inflating the money supply and artificially controlling interest rates is morally wrong.
      i. It's a form of taking from one and giving to another in a deceptive way and is a violation of the 8th and 9th commandments: do not steal and do not lie.
      ii. The resulting recession/depression is in one respect the moral consequence of bad economic decisions. As we were all told as children: a lie will eventually catch up to you—and when it does, it won't be pretty.
      iii. In a depression, basic stewardship becomes much more difficult: as we said before, the division of labor suffers, productivity suffers, marriages and families suffer, churches suffer, and so on.
   B. In bust situations, you have two options:
      i. The honest thing to do is to let the bad businesses fail, let others pick up the pieces, and let everyone freely start re-building on a better foundation.

ii. The dishonest thing? To deny that inflationary monetary policies and low interest rates caused the problem, and instead continue to inflate the money supply. But that's not the worst possibility.

7. What made the 1930's Depression Great?
   A. A simple comparison of the 1920–21 Depression with the Great Depression of the 1930's is instructive.
      i. In 1920, as soon as the Fed realized the country was in a depression, it pushed up interest rates to a record high and stopped inflating the money supply.
         a. Government itself did very little: no bailouts, no work programs, nothing. Although there was a depression, it wasn't great. Within a year, the economy purged off the bad business decisions and started growing again.
         b. Yet, no one learned the lesson. By the early 1920's a new inflationary monetary policy and new lower interest rates started the cycle again. And so the bubble started to grow and grow. In 1929, it burst.
      ii. In 1930, government officials thought they could start intervening to fix things faster.
         a. The Hoover administration and the Fed continued to inflate the money supply, prop up wages, passed new tariffs, raised taxes, and started spending on government programs. When FDR game into office in 1933, he simply did more of the same.
         b. What was the result? The Great Depression that lasted from 1929 all the way to 1941.

1) In fact, if you take out the government sponsored spending of WWII, the Great Depression really didn't end until after the war was over.
2) Why did it end then? For four years people had been saving and saving since there wasn't much to buy: so the savings rate of real wealth was enormous. It was these savings that were the foundation of the post-war economic growth.

iii. The solution to our second mystery? Why did the Great Depression last for at least 12 years, if not longer, when the depression just a decade before lasted around 18 months? The Great Depression was caused by government intervention like the United States had never seen before.

B. Ironically, it was the Great Depression that pushed the US into even greater government intervention in spite of the fact that it was government intervention that got it there in the first place!

i. Contrary to popular opinion, both Presidents Hoover and Roosevelt did very similar things to combat the depression. In fact, Roosevelt simply pushed things further down the path Hoover had started out on.

ii. Here are a few key interventionist actions that demonstrate again our points about the basic problems of interventionism:

a. *Artificially Prop up Wages*: After the crash in 1929, then-President Herbert Hoover worked with business leaders to keep wages artificially high. Instead of lowering wages when revenues fell, businesses were forced to keep wages high and just lay off workers they couldn't afford.

1) The result: unemployment shot up to 28% by 1933.
2) What happened in the 1920 depression? Government did nothing, wages fell 20% but unemployment only rose to 11% in 1921 and was back down to 2.4% by 1923. The free market fixed the problems caused by government intervention.

b. *Increase Taxes*: Both Hoover and Roosevelt increased taxes, increased government spending on programs designed to stop the depression, and ran budget deficits in order to pay for everything. Let's take one tax level as an example. If you made $20,000 a year, here's how your income tax would have increased from 1931 to 1934:
   1) 1931–10% of $20,000
   2) 1932–16% of $20,000
   3) 1934–19% of $20,000

c. *Increase Spending on a lot of Government Programs to Influence the Economy*:
   1) Federal government spending increased 2.5x from $3.8 billion in 1929 to $9.17 billion in 1936. This spending was intended to "get the economy back on its feet" but really just perpetuated the problems that come from increased government

intervention: unemployment and weak economic growth. Unemployment in the US never statistically recovered to 1920 levels until the US entered WWII.

2) Billions went to fund various government-run programs that were supposed to fix the problem. These are collectively known as The New Deal, something that many historians claim pulled us out of the Depression.
   (A) These programs did not do this, but instead are watershed instances of government intervention pushing the US closer toward socialism.
   (B) The New Deal ensured that the US moved further away from a free market economy and stepped closer toward the command and control end of the spectrum. Here are just a few examples:
      (i) The National Recovery Administration required all businesses within an industry to establish uniform prices, thereby removing the possibility of competition. The result: tens of thousands of small businesses had to shut down since they could no longer compete with big businesses in their industry.
      (ii) Although people were going hungry during the Depression, in order to try to raise agriculture prices, the Agricultural Adjustment Administration actually *paid* farmers to destroy their own crops and animals.

(a) Cotton farmers were paid to plow under 10 million acres of cotton; hog farmers were paid to kill 6 million pigs (most of which became fertilizer instead of food); and thousands of acres of tobacco, oranges, and oats were burned, as well as many other crops.

(b) Talk about the bizarre things that happen when the government tries to control the economy!

(iii) Since there were so many unemployed in the nation, why not have the government hire a lot of them? So the Works Progress Administration spent hundreds of millions of dollars hiring over 8 million people to build roads, dams, bridges, public buildings, etc.

(a) Of course, the basic economic problem here is that billions of dollars are redirected out of the private sector (where they could have been used to create profitable businesses) and instead used once, then lost in specific construction projects.

(b) Sure, one has a bridge, a building, a road, or a dam—but the country doesn't have additional *businesses* which can continue to live on and pay people after the government job is finished. If needed, those same bridges, roads, dams could have been built out of surpluses when the local community wanted them to be built.

(c) Such government redirection of funds may look good in the short term, but does nothing to solve the basic economic problem: how to produce goods or services that people will want or need over the long-haul. In other words, a business that can grow.

3) To sum it all up, looking back over almost a decade of government intervention, the Secretary of the Treasury said in 1939: "We have tried spending money. We are spending more than we have ever spent before and it does not work.... We have never made good on our promises.... I say after eight years of this Administration we have just as much unemployment as when we started.... And an enormous debt to boot!" –Henry Morgenthau, Jr., Secretary of the Treasury

8. Closing Thoughts

A. So why did we spend an entire lesson on early twentieth-century US history? It's because the distance of time gives us the ability to see the consequences of certain economic decisions.

B. It also enables us to see where one of the greatest free market economies of the world took a serious wrong turn down the path of government intervention. In the next lesson, we will see just what some of the consequences of those choices were.

C. But in terms of our ability to be good stewards with what God has given us, we need to remember two points:
   i. Intentional inflation is a dishonest monetary policy that results in the wholesale destruction of wealth across an entire nation. It must be fought tooth and nail by Christians who understand that maintaining the long-term value of their money is necessary for being a good steward and building up the Kingdom of God.
   ii. Inflation leads inevitably toward national recessions and depressions that bankrupt businesses, wipe out savings and investments, and consistently lead to even more government intervention. This has the effect over time of driving a nation closer and closer toward socialism and the inevitable poverty that must always accompany a command and control economic system.

MULTIPLE CHOICE

1. What is money?
   a. A means of exchange.
   b. A unit of account.
   c. A store of value.
   d. All of the above.
2. ________ coordinate production and business decisions over time.
   a. Money multipliers
   b. Inflationary monetary policies
   c. Interest rates
   d. Economic calculations

3. An inflationary monetary policy ends up creating a ________ cycle in an economy.
   a. bust/boom
   b. boom/boom
   c. boom/bust
   d. bust/bust
4. What was the cause of the Great Depression?
   a. The stock market crash.
   b. An inflationary money supply and low interest rates.
   c. Government fiscal policies.
   d. A constricted money supply.
5. What made the Great Depression last for over a decade?
   a. Widespread unemployment.
   b. The free market.
   c. Far-reaching government intervention.
   d. Inflationary monetary policies.

SHORT ANSWER

1. Compare and contrast the Depression of the 1930's and the "Great" Recession of the early twenty-first century (2008 and forward).

2. What are the moral problems with inflation?

3. Why do government spending programs designed to "get the economy going" ultimately fail?

DISCUSSION

1. What are some of the ways you have seen inflation hurt you or ones you know through its effects? How is inflation bad for the church?
2. Why is government spending so ineffective at stopping a recession or depression?
3. The Bible talks about "honest money" in many places. What are some ways that you see dishonesty in our monetary system, and what are possible ways to fix it?

FOR FURTHER STUDY

Honest Money—Gary North
Basic Economics, 3rd Ed.—Carson & Cleveland—Chapter 8
Foundations of Economics—Ritenour—Chapter 13
Prosperity and Poverty—Beisner—Chapters 9–10
The Politically Incorrect Guide to the Great Depression and the New Deal–Murphy

Multiple choice answers: 1.d 2.c 3.c 4.b 5.c

10

The Welfare and Corporate States of America: The Costs of Redistribution

MESSAGE INTRODUCTION

Government intervention greatly affects American society by redistributing the wealth of the nation. In this lesson, we'll look at the nature of welfarism and its impact on society; at the Biblical perspective of charity; at the growth of corporatism; and at the implications of heavy taxation and borrowing.

SCRIPTURE READING

1 Samuel 8

LEARNING OBJECTIVES

1. To understand the nature of welfarism and corporatism.
2. To see what happens when these policies are pursued.
3. To recognize the scope and weight of fiscal policy on being a steward.

QUOTATIONS

The problem with socialism is that you eventually run out of other people's money.

—Margaret Thatcher

LECTURE OUTLINE

1. In the last lesson, we talked about the many government programs brought about by the New Deal. Let's now consider one of the biggest programs to come from that era: the Works Progress Administration (WPA).
   A. There was high unemployment during the Depression, so the Roosevelt administration tried to implement a government solution for putting people back to work. The result was the WPA, a mammoth agency with 8 million employees, so to speak, that was involved with constructing roads, dams, bridges, parks, buildings and all sorts of public infrastructure.
   B. On the surface, that sounds great. But let's ask a few questions to get below the surface:
      i. Who benefits from this program?
         a. Obviously the unemployed men who are suddenly getting a paycheck.
         b. Next, those construction companies that win the big new projects and then get lots of subsidized labor.
         c. And, of course, the politicians whose districts and states receive the fruits of the construction done in them.
      ii. But let's also ask, who loses? This is not a market-based decision, but one made by central bureaucrats and political appointees. Someone has to decide where the money goes.
         a. If you're a normal construction worker working in the market, it's now flooded with all these subsidized men getting money from the government. That certainly messes

up the pay structure and market dynamics you depend on to feed you and your family. (After all, not everyone was out of work during the depression. Even at the time of highest unemployment, three out of four people still had jobs.)

b. You also lose if you work for one of the construction companies that doesn't get the new bids due to lack of political connections.
c. Or, if you are an opposing politician and don't have big public works projects to give to your state, then you lose out against your opponent who can get those favors.
d. Ultimately, however, it's the nation that loses because the government is re-directing hundreds of millions of taxpayer dollars for construction programs and buildings that the market doesn't call for. That money would instead have gone into the market to create new businesses and jobs. Because resources are directed away from their most highly valued uses as determined by the market, society as a whole is less productive and therefore people are able to obtain fewer goods with which they can satisfy their ends.

iii. But that's not the worst thing about the WPA and other New Deal programs. In the long run, they create a mindset that the government is ultimately responsible for the personal welfare of individual citizens. This has three disastrous results:

a. For those 8 million citizens who were employed by the program, we've constructed a form of *welfarism* where they are now dependent on the state for their income.
b. And for those construction companies who win those bids, whether in outright competition or through political favors, they're really getting the same kind of government help, so we have a type of welfarism we will call *corporatism*.
c. Together, they begin to lead people to believe that how much wealth they acquire is no longer dependent on how productive they are, what good stewards they are, or what kind of work they do. Now the distribution of money is determined politically.

iv. Don't forget our North Star principle: what does this mindset mean for stewardship?

2. Welfarism is a mindset and philosophy that is a significant departure from the Biblical view.
   A. We need to remember that government is created by God and serves a purpose. It should have the necessary funds it needs to fulfill its God-given calling of protecting life and property.
      i. But what we've seen in the twentieth and twenty-first centuries is the growth of the perspective that a nation's wealth is to be redistributed by the state for a variety of reasons, including political, social, economic, and others.
   B. The introduction of the New Deal was the official start of the *welfare state* in the United States. Although there had been government programs

before in prior administrations, the New Deal took these programs to an unheard of new level.

i. The welfare perspective is this: the government can and should provide for the material and intellectual well-being of its people by controlling and directing the economy.

ii. Prior to this, government tended only to step forward to take more control during wartime. But now, in the context of peace, the central government took control of all aspects of the economy.

iii. This involved a new interpretation of 'well-being' or 'welfare,' that was now applied to government poverty relief, old-age pensions, healthcare, education, housing, unemployment, subsidies, and many other things.

C. This is a significant departure from the mindset that guided our country from its founding at least until the early twentieth century.

i. During the first century of the Republic, citizens understood that the primary role of the government was to protect life and property. It was then up to individuals to determine their lives.

ii. The general goal was to restrict Government involvement in private life, especially in terms of government spending and taxation. The founding fathers and those who followed them had come from countries with strong government involvement in the economy via taxing and spending. They had seen the damage it did first hand, and wanted little of it.

D. But welfarism is also a departure from the Biblical view.

i. The Bible teaches it's the responsibility of the church and individuals to provide charity.
   a. When solutions to poverty are local, people are closer to the problem and can monitor responsibility and provide personal accountability; after all, sinful decisions are a basic cause of poverty.
   b. It also means people are giving from real savings, so they are not providing more than they can afford.

ii. The Bible links together work and income. Paul says, *"If anyone is not willing to work, let him not eat"* (2 Thess. 3:10).

iii. In fact, the Bible sees vocational work—a man or woman's calling—as central to his or her meaning as a person.

iv. Most importantly, the Bible connects charity with the gospel message.
   a. Jesus said, *"The Spirit of the Lord is upon me, because he has anointed me to proclaim good news to the poor. He has sent me to proclaim liberty to the captives and recovering of sight to the blind, to set at liberty those who are oppressed..."* (Luke 4:18).
   b. If someone is in poverty because of his sin, and charity comes without the gospel message and a call to repentance, then the real reason for his poverty is never addressed. We could call this practice the 'prodigal son preservation society.'

E. All of these views were replaced in the early twentieth century with the economic philosophy that the government is responsible for providing for the material and intellectual needs of its people, especially when they are in distress.

i. This philosophy arose only after a period of great prosperity brought about by the extraordinary growth of the free market in eighteenth- and nineteenth-century England, America & Europe.
ii. Yet this philosophy is a denial of some basic economic and Biblical principles:
    a. It does not believe there is real scarcity and a curse on the ground. Instead, it believes the problems of production have been solved and the real question is one of *distribution.* In other words, we have plenty of goods and services, but they are not being distributed evenly amongst people.
        1) Of course, what happens if you stop focusing on production? There eventually isn't anything to distribute.
    2. It does not see the link between work, production, and creation of wealth. Instead, it sees wealth as something that just exists and so must be evenly distributed. Its view of goods and services is like a pie, where everyone should get a small slice. But if the pie is not being grown, then we end up having to slice the pie in smaller and smaller pieces.
    c. Finally, it believes the government has the right to control every individual's private property and ultimately determine what to do with it. Notice the socialist philosophy that

supports the welfarist economic mindset: ultimately the government can tell the individual how much he can keep of his own property.

1) This is the way it is in the United States. How do we know this? Stop paying your property taxes and see who will take your house. Stop paying your income taxes and see who will take your bank account as well as your ability to labor. You get the picture.

3. Since welfarism is just a form of government intervention, it ends up creating economic problems we've seen before.
   A. Remember that government can't produce anything; it can only restrict, consume and redirect. So where does the government get the money to re-distribute? It takes it from those who are producing.
   B. Some individuals want to redistribute other people's money for their own purposes, so they pull the levers of the government to force those other people to give their money either to themselves or to someone else.
   C. This causes the following economic problems:
      i. As the government takes more and more money from those who are productive, it confuses economic calculation in the market. After all, the government is now taking a significant percentage of what people are producing then re-directing it, so there's no economic rhyme or reason as to where the money is going.
      ii. In this case, taking from the more productive in society and giving to the less productive means the government is determining how a signifi-

cant percentage of a nation's wealth should be used. In the case of welfarism, it ensures money will be used for consumption instead of savings, production and job creation.

D. How much money does the US government take and redistribute?
   i. The amount of money spent just on pensions, welfare, and healthcare from 1934 (the year the Social Security Act passed) to 2008 (the last year we have actual numbers reported) was *$45 trillion.* (That number is adjusted for inflation by equalizing everything to 2005 dollars). That's a lot of money that was forcibly taken out of production and used for consumption.
E. But the basic problems of intervention apply directly to the development of the welfare state.
   i. Initial intervention in the market always fails to achieve its ultimate ends, so more intervention is applied. Every government program is testimony to this. For example, the US spent $800 million on welfare in 1930; in 2008 it spent $459 *billion.* That's an increase of 57,300%![†]
   ii. As intervention grows throughout a nation's economy, it slowly but inevitably pushes that nation toward greater socialism. The closer it gets to socialism, the closer it moves toward poverty.
   iii. These policies create enormous, constantly increasing groups of people either partially or completely dependent on government redistribution for survival, as opposed to their own work.

a. This is harmful to them as men and women made in God's image who, according to the cultural mandate, need to steward the creation according to their vocation in order to have significance.
b. Many who receive this support stop seeing the connection between work, production and income. This group relies on the government to provide for their basic needs so their own economic compass is twisted, hindering themselves from ever being able to prosper.
c. Government programs designed to help poverty *actually increase it*. It is a simple economic concept: if you give a subsidy (or money) to someone for doing something, they will be economically inclined to do more of it.
    1) This has terrible side-effects on individuals who get the money. It is like the drug that your doctor gives you to help with the flu not only makes you sicker, but also gives you pneumonia!
    2) It is the logical corollary of everything we've seen so far: divorce work and production from income and it destroys those who are receiving it.
d. These policies pile an ever-heavier load on the productive members of society. Producers can only provide so much without buckling under at the margins. We'll look at specific numbers in a minute, but the main point is this: government redistribution will

eventually run out of money. This is always the inevitable end of government intervention and socialism.

F. But isn't it right to help people, no matter what the source?
   i. It is right for us to help people who are truly in need, but as individuals or as the church, not as the government. When the government gets involved in taking care of people it is disastrous both for the one taken from and the one given to.
   ii. In regard to those who have money taken from them for redistribution, it's a violation of the 8th commandment. Not only is it morally wrong, it's also an economic waste: the divorce of private property from its rightful owners ends necessarily in the squandering of the property at government hands. After all, true economic calculation is impossible for the government bureaucrat.
   iii. As for those who receive monetary help from the government, they become dependent and don't have their real spiritual and moral issues addressed. They and their children are consistently consigned to an ongoing poverty.
      a. Just look at the huge tracts of government housing in any city where 2nd and 3rd generation recipients are generally on welfare, unemployed, and unmarried. This is not stereotypical—these are the hard facts and the brutal results of a Welfare State. This is a terrible place to be consigned.

G. But surely if the government stopped helping people the church couldn't do the same thing?
  i. Just as it has taken decades to get us this far into the welfare state, it can't be changed overnight. However, if the government slowly stopped redistributing to people two things would happen:
    a. Those who are capable of work would seek a way to support themselves.
    b. Those who legitimately were not capable would be taken care of by organizations truly able to meet all their needs.

H. In sum, welfare is not only bad economically and wrong morally, it is disastrous on those receiving it. All these things are related, of course—but generational dependency on the state is the exact opposite of Biblical stewardship. It ensures that whole groups of people will not be fulfilled vocationally or be able to employ their God-given abilities. Ongoing receiving is not producing, and we are created in God's image to produce.

4. There is another form of government spending that happens when particular industries, businesses, and special interests turn not to the market to help grow their business, but to the state: *Corporatism*.
  A. Corporatism usually happens in one of two ways.
    i. If a business is not able to raise the money it needs in the marketplace, it can go to the state to get projects, subsidies, loans and investment capital.

   ii. A business can also use the state to regulate away their competition. Some businesses (usually larger ones) work to have laws passed that give them an unfair advantage in the marketplace.

B. Which industries in the United States are the most corporatist? They are also all represented on the President's cabinet: Banking (Treasury), Agriculture, Defense, Energy, Education, Transportation, Labor, Interior, Commerce, Healthcare, Security, and so on. (There are now even "czars" and a multitude of lesser-known appointees to manage these ever-burgeoning corporate interests).
   i. The result is that the political system is about electing people or influencing those already elected in order to get a bigger piece of the pie or to control more of the market.
   ii. There has been significant growth of corporatism in the US since the Civil War, to the point that an enormous amount of business is linked to government purse strings in some way or another. Of course, those purse strings can become bridles.

C. Since corporatism is just another form of interventionism, it too suffers from the same kinds of problems:
   i. It confuses the market and the economic calculation of businesses. It is actually a throwback to royal charters when the king had businesses that received his special favor and prospered as a result. Those who still try to play by free market rules are at a significant disadvantage.
   ii. The bureaucrat/politician replaces the entrepreneur as to where and how to use capital.

a. But it's impossible for the government to have the information and ability to know what to do with that capital to make it most effective, since their decisions are divorced from market feedback.

b. This means that businesses that get government money are the ones with either the best political connections or the best contract-getting skills, not necessarily the ones that would be chosen by real consumers or investors in the market.

iii. This allows politically connected, but less productive and efficient businesses to thrive based on the work of productive businesses (those that pay the taxes being redistributed.) It eventually can drive those less-favored businesses out of the market or industry.

iv. Since production has now been separated from the market, then huge amounts of money are wasted on projects and industries. We know the stories; we read about them all the time in the news. But these happen to be waves across the surface of government rivers, most of which is unseen by the majority of the population.

5. It costs the United States a lot of money to support its Welfare and Corporate States.

A. If we look at total spending to include federal, state and local government, we see a gargantuan increase in government spending over the past century.

i. In 1910, the government spent about 8% of the nation's Gross Domestic Product (GDP) at $43 billion dollars.[†] This means the government was spending $8 for every $100 produced. (GDP is a number that supposedly approximates what a nation produces in a year. You will hear it talked about a lot. Of course, it's not really possible to measure production with a single numerical value, but it's a generally-accepted way to look at the productive output of a country, so it does have some use in comparisons.)

ii. In 2008, however, the government spent about 37% of the nation's GDP to the tune of $4.9 trillion dollars.[†] That's over a third of the nation's productive capacity being redistributed! (And considering the economy did grow substantially during that period, it's an exceptional amount of purchasing power being taken from the nation.)

B. What is the money being spent on? The truth is, it's difficult to track where that much money really ends up, but we know that in 2008, the US spent the following on its Welfare State: [†]

i. $774 billion on Pensions (Social Security, etc.)
ii. $835 billion on Healthcare (Medicare, etc.)
iii. $791 billion on Education
iv. $439 billion on Welfare
v. Added up, that's nearly 3 trillion dollars being re-directed and re-distributed. That's a whole lot of money.

C. Corporate spending, unfortunately, is even more complex since it is not always clear how the money is changing hands, and who is getting what.

i. But some areas remain dominant: Defense, Transportation, Agriculture, Energy, Environment, and so forth (remember the cabinets and czars). Here is what our government spent on these areas in 2008:

a. $666 billion in defense

b. $240 billion in transportation

c. $412 billion in "Other Spending" which includes Agriculture, Energy, Environment, Cultural, and Research

ii. It's true that some of these services we would consider necessary to protecting ourselves and providing for some basic government services (such as judicial, etc.). But the majority of the expenditures, including defense, are wrapped up tightly in corporate interests, be it the construction industry, defense contracting, the energy industry, and so forth.

iii. In most of these cases, there are free market solutions that would be far more advantageous to the taxpayer and the system as a whole.

D. Spending almost never goes in reverse. This is the rule of government intervention in the economy: it will always demand more and more money, and more and more intervention because it cannot achieve the goals it seeks. This is an economic principle that real numbers consistently demonstrate. (Just try to name a major government department that is growing smaller.)

E. Government economic intervention becomes more and more costly in terms of lost production and misallocated wealth, to the point that it will bankrupt a nation.

6. If all these government programs are spending money, then they have to get that money somewhere. Since government cannot produce anything, there are two main sources for its money: *taxation* and *borrowing*. Here's a quick comparison between two periods in our nation's history:
   A. Taxation in the Early Republic
      i. A series of rebellions against various excise taxes (taxes on goods produced for sale within a country) actually started the American Revolution.
      ii. Taxes were always suspect by the early Americans. They had suffered under Britain's steep (to them) taxes for too long. They knew taxes were necessary, but only enough to support a government that protected life and private property. Compared to today, the taxes were exceptionally minimal.
   B. Taxation in the Twentieth and Twenty-First Centuries
      i. Introduction of more and more programs required more and more money to pay for them. Taxes to support a welfare state with an expanding pool of dependents are necessarily heavy.
      ii. A barrage of new taxes appeared at the start of the twentieth century: income taxes, estate taxes, corporate taxes, investment taxes, and on and on. Many of these would never have been allowed in the early republic.
         a. For example, the federal income tax was declared unconstitutional over and over until it was passed as the 16th Amendment

in 1913. The Constitution had not allowed government to tax people's labor, but the British Parliament first realized how much money could be made this way in the nineteenth century, so the Americans eventually followed suit.

b. The income tax was designed as a *progressive* tax. Progressive taxes increase the percentage of tax someone must pay simply because they have a higher income. It is inherently disproportionate. (This is opposed to a *flat* tax, which is basically a single rate applied evenly to all.)
    1) A progressive tax is a violation of basic fairness: it treats people differently based on the amount of wealth they produce. Why should someone who makes more money pay more taxes? Are they being protected better than others? Or using more government services? The US has had progressive taxes for so long that most people don't even consider the inherent unfairness of them.
    2) Of course, progressive taxes are also a violation of the 8th commandment. The goal of taking more from one than another is to redistribute that surplus to someone else.

C. For perspective, total government revenues (Federal, State, and Local) in 2008 was $4.3 trillion dollars.[‡] That's a lot of money taken out of the market and put into bureaucratic hands.

7. A nation that will not tax enough to cover what it's spending (or actually cut the spending) must *borrow* the difference.
   A. This is particularly dangerous for a government that has no means of producing anything. It can only pay back what it borrows through additional taxation.
   B. Since our nation has been spending more than it has produced for many years, we have accumulated a mind-boggling amount of federal debt. It continues to grow quickly, as these debt numbers reveal:
      i. FY 2008—$10 trillion
      ii. FY 2009—$11.9 trillion
      iii. FY 2010—$13.5 trillion
      iv. FY 2011—$14.8 trillion
      v. FY 2012—$16.4 trillion†
   C. The Bible has lot to say about debt, but the most succinct is this: *The borrower is the slave of the lender* (Prov. 22:7).
   D. The Biblical principle is obvious: debt is like heavy chains that economically constrict a person as well as a nation and prevent them from growing. It is yet another way that stewardship is thwarted.

8. Closing
   A. The twin paths of welfarism and corporatism lead far away from the free market. They are dark paths of interventionism that a nation must beware.
   B. Our nation's current levels of spending, taxation, and borrowing are a direct result of our interventionist economy. Unless they are stopped, they will grow until they choke out all good growth.

C. Interventionism results in a form of slavery for those inside the society. Slavery to those who are receiving, and slavery to those who have to work ever more days, weeks and months just to support those not working.
D. Ultimately, welfarism and corporatism are the paths to socialism and poverty. As we will see in the next lesson, there are serious consequences for Christians if a nation goes down these paths.

MULTIPLE CHOICE

1. The welfare perspective is that the government can and should provide for the material and intellectual well-being of its people by _______ the economy.
   a. assisting and helping
   b. ignoring and leaving alone
   c. controlling and directing
   d. seizing and taxing

2. The Bible teaches it's the responsibility of the _______ to provide charity.
   a. church alone
   b. business sector
   c. church and individuals
   d. government

3. In regard to those who have money taken from them for redistribution, it's a violation of the _______.
   a. 7th Commandment
   b. 8th Commandment
   c. 9th Commandment
   d. 10th Commandment

4. In corporatism, the ______ replaces the entrepreneur in determining where and how to use capital.
   a. board of directors
   b. bureaucrat/politician
   c. majority stockholder
   d. central planner

5. ______ taxes increase the percentage of tax someone must pay simply because they have a higher income.
   a. Permissive
   b. Progressive
   c. Flat
   d. Direct

SHORT ANSWER

1. What has been the effect on the church ever since the government took over the role of providing welfare to the poor?

2. What are some of the bad consequences of corporatism?

3. How does high taxation effect stewardship? Name some specific situations where you see the results of this.

DISCUSSION

1. Talk about some examples of welfarism or corporatism that you have seen or know about from first-hand experience. What are the results?

2. It rubs some Christians the wrong way when it is suggested that the government cut back and even remove itself from the position of taking care of its citizens, particularly the poor. But if these programs ultimately hurt more than help people, what is the moral obligation of Christians? Furthermore, what can Christians do to replace ineffective government services with gospel-centered charity?
3. Many businesses are extremely dependent on government contracts. Is this a good long-term solution for either these businesses or for government? One old saying is: "He who pays the piper calls the tune." Does this have moral implications for businesses that are dependent on the government?

FOR FURTHER STUDY

Basic Economics, 3rd Ed.—Carson & Cleveland—Chapters 19–20
Foundations of Economics—Ritenour—Chapter 16
Unmasking the Sacred Lies—Cleveland—Chapters 2, 8
Biblical Economics—Sproul—Chapter 8

[†] www.usgovernmentspending.com
[‡] www.usgovernmentrevenue.com

Multiple choice answers: 1.c 2.c 3.b 4.b 5.b

11

Economics Has Consequences: The Real Effects of Sin

MESSAGE INTRODUCTION

Sin has very different consequences depending on the structure of economic systems. In this lesson, we'll look at a comparison between North and South Korea; at the way economies take sin into account; at revolutionary socialism in practice; at the regulatory environment created by government intervention; and at questions of poverty and greed within free markets.

SCRIPTURE READING

Deuteronomy 28

LEARNING OBJECTIVES

1. To understand that an economic system is only as effective as it takes sin into account.
2. To see that there are radical differences in the ways individual men and women live in different economic systems.
3. To recognize that economic ideas have consequences for day-to-day life.

QUOTATIONS

> *A great disaster had befallen Russia: Men have forgotten God; that's why all this has happened.*
>
> —Alexander Solzhenitsyn

LECTURE OUTLINE

1. Introduction—a 60-year Foot Race
   A. After all we've studied, the time has come to look at the true consequences of economic systems on the real men and women who live within them. As always, let's keep our North Star principle in front of us and ask: what is the impact these economic choices have on Biblical stewardship?
   B. It is interesting to compare the economic outcomes of two countries that essentially started life at the same time in the twentieth century: North and South Korea.
      i. Here's a brief history:
         a. At one time, Korea was a unified peninsula. It was taken over by the Japanese in 1905 and controlled by them until the end of WWII. In 1945, the Soviet Union took control of the northern half of the peninsula and began work at setting up a socialist command and control government and economy. Their ultimate goal was to control the entire peninsula, but the United States supervised the Southern half.
         b. The next three years of political struggle ended in the establishment in 1948 of a socialist dictatorship in North Korea and a

democratic, generally free market economy in South Korea.

c. By 1950, due to the withdrawal of American troops and other political developments, Stalin thought the South was vulnerable and encouraged an invasion. The result was the Korean War in which American forces and the South Koreans won a victory for the South in 1953 by pushing the North back to its original borders.

d. Since that time, North Korea has pursued a highly controlled socialist economy. The government controls all its industries, all its vocations, all its production, everything.

e. On the other hand, South Korea has pursued a generally free market economy with the government intervening in the economy to a far lesser degree. In contrast, we can say industries are free, production is free, vocations are free.

ii. As a result, Korea is a fascinating comparison of two different economies starting from the same point and running a side-by-side race for six decades.

a. If you look at a recent satellite photo of the entire peninsula taken at night, it reveals a radical difference.

1) North Korea is literally living in darkness as a result of its socialist economic decisions. There's not enough electricity to power the country for an entire day, so they have blackouts at night.

2) South Korea, on the other hand, is a brightly-lit market economy that is impressive in its prosperity.

iii. In just 60 years, there has been such a radical divergence between the two countries that one is at the top of the world's economic scale and the other is at the bottom.

a. The South has food surpluses both through its own farming and its international trade; the North struggles through ongoing famines and regular starvation, often requiring food supplies from International and South Korean governments and charities just to survive.

b. The South has full and thriving cities with bustling streets and full buildings; the North has empty and dead cities with empty streets and empty buildings.

c. The South has renowned robotics, aerospace, and biotechnology industries and is one of the top 10 exporters and importers in the world; the North struggles to maintain its burgeoning military at the expense of all other industries.

d. The South is one of the fastest growing and richest economies in the world, ranked in the top 20 with more than $20,000 in per capita income; the North is one of the poorest countries, in the bottom 20 with less than $2,000 in per capita income.

iv. And what is the effect on Christianity and stewardship?

a. South Korea is one of the most Christian nations in the world.
   1) A 2005 census put the number of Christians in South Korea at almost 14 million in this nation of 24 million people. That's nearly 60% Christian. Seoul boasts 11 of the 12 largest Christian congregations in the world, with one Assemblies of God church having 1,000,000 members. (Really!)
   2) Every year South Korea sends tens of thousands of missionaries all over the world. After the US, South Korea is the second largest missionary sending nation. South Korea's market based economy has fueled incredible conquests for the Kingdom of God both internally and world-wide.
b. North Korea, on the other hand, is one of the most atheistic nations in the world.
   1) It is considered one of the greatest national persecutors of Christians. Outlawed by the government, Christians are imprisoned, tortured, and killed. Right now, there are approximately 50 to 70 thousand Christians detained in North Korean prisons. The Voice of the Martyrs regularly reports on the horrific situation Christians face in North Korea.

v. This quick comparison shows us the extreme difference in results between a socialist economy and a generally free market economy.

a. But this isn't the only case: compare Taiwan or Hong Kong and mainland China (especially 30 years ago before China started its market reforms); compare the former East Germany and West Germany; compare Cuba before and after Castro. And there are many other examples of the dire failures of socialism and the triumphs of the free market.
b. Socialism, both in its revolutionary as well as its gradual interventionist ways, always ends in the persecution of Christians, the growth of Satan's kingdom, and the denial of Biblical stewardship, not to mention great poverty and distress for all those living inside those economies.
c. In the same way, the free market in countries with relatively mild interventionism leads toward the freedom of Christians, growth of the Kingdom, and the flowering of Biblical stewardship.

2. One key question determines everything about the consequences of an economic system: how does an economy take into account man's sin?
   A. The reality of sin in every person must never be forgotten. Those economic systems that recognize man's basic sinfulness are consistently free because they take steps to protect men from other men. Those systems that deny man's sinfulness are consistently enslaved since they were designed by a few men to control all others.

B. Here is the irony: socialist systems start with the assumption that most men (especially poor men) are basically good, but misguided and exploited by the wealthy. All they need is education, leadership and organization to create a *utopia* here on earth. This socialist utopia is a nation of plenty that has been freed from poverty. It has also been freed from Christianity and all its doctrines of heaven and hell.
   i. Never underestimate the utopian vision even if it comes in different versions.
      a. It is the rationale behind all the work that socialists do to advance their causes. They have been able to capture the hearts and minds of millions and millions of people with a vision of "heaven on earth." This thinking continues to be used even here in the United States where people are promised that the government can give them 'a better tomorrow.'
      b. This is why it is necessary to banish Christianity from their system: Christ teaches that man will never be perfected on this earth, the poor will always be with us, and the only utopia possible is in heaven above.
   ii. The question of the poor or the exploited worker has often been at the forefront of socialist economic endeavors.
      a. Sometimes this has been there to mask someone else taking control—as in the case of Lenin or Mao.

b. Sometimes it has been a legitimate, if not well thought out, concern—as in the case of gradual socialists such as Franklin Delano Roosevelt.

c. In both cases, however, it's always someone acting on behalf of others to setup a new economic system that is somehow going to solve their problems and usher in a utopia. Yet history shows it is not plenty that comes with socialism, but poverty; and in most cases, it is not heaven that is established on earth, but a type of hell.

3. Visions of Utopia and Cities of Hell: *Revolutionary Socialism* in Practice

   A. Let's begin with the consequences of revolutionary socialism.

      i. The most famous revolutionary socialist was Karl Marx, a German economist who took up residence in England in the mid-nineteenth century. He called his form of socialism *communism*. It was the most influential economic movement in the twentieth century, and still remains highly influential in the twenty-first century.

         a. Marx argued that free market economies (which he called capitalist) should be violently overthrown with much bloodshed; socialist economies should then be set up in their places.

         b. Many people do not realize that Communist socialism starts with economics and builds its system from economic premises. Marx's economics are confused and often illogical, but they are still followed today with varying degrees in many parts of the world.

c. Marx hated God, and intentionally designed a political and economic system that would dethrone Him from heaven. All his disciples who tried to implement his visions wanted to do the same. These are the true atheist systems, designed to be the polar opposite of anything Christian.

ii. Why is it so important for an economic system to war against God? It always comes back to whom the world is being stewarded for: God or Satan. The revolutionary socialists were very consistent in their thinking.

a. Socialists do not believe in the fall of man or sin, in the cultural mandate, or in vocational stewardship. They consistently deny these ideas and work off an economic system that ignores or flatly contradicts them. What is the result?

b. As we have seen before, a socialist political and economic system ultimately removes all freedom from individual men to work, raise families, live and worship as they choose. This is instead the role of the State and its central planners.

iii. Which countries have implemented revolutionary socialist systems either currently or sometime in their past? Russia, China, North Korea, Cuba, Vietnam, Cambodia, Angola, Ethiopia, among many others.

a. Every one of these countries remained a picture of poverty as long as they were pursuing a socialist economy. It was only in trying to implement some market conditions that these countries started to grow economically. But while still socialist, they were economic disasters.

B. Economic calculation is impossible in a socialist economy. Central planners will inevitably misallocate a nation's land, labor, and capital because they deny the role of the individual consumer and importance of the market, especially its freedom. The logical results are ongoing economic depression and stagnation. This is what happens:

i. There is a shortage of basic goods.

a. Stores in these socialist countries regularly had bare shelves or, more bizarrely, were filled with things no one actually wanted. Lines in front of stores are not an uncommon sight in socialist countries. People wait not to buy the newest gadget but to get their ration of groceries.

b. This shortage is the combined result of maximum and minimum prices, government control of the means of production, and lack of market feedback.

c. This mismanagement of production eventually ends in famines.

1) There were many famines in Russia caused by Soviet policies, such as in 1921 & 1922, 1932 & 1933, 1946 & 1947; these

famines resulted in the deaths of approximately 17 million people.

2) China's Great Famine from 1958 to 1961 was a direct result of Mao's ludicrous economic and agricultural ideas; it resulted in the deaths of between 35–45 million people.
3) North Korea continues to have famines to this day, all a result of its extreme socialist policies.
4) This kind of famine in the modern world can only happen as a result of government action. Socialism ultimately results in starvation for its people.

ii. Socialist nations are technologically primitive.

a. Since there isn't a market to encourage growth, then socialist economies are always "looking over the fence" to see what the market economy is creating and mimicking it in terms of products.
b. Nevertheless, it's impossible to keep up. Western tourists who visited the Soviet Union and Eastern bloc countries after the fall of the Berlin Wall were amazed at what they saw: old cars, old buildings, old clothing—as if the countries were somehow stuck in a time warp.
c. Since the free market is ignored, the black market grows to meet the needs of the people. All socialist countries that deny free markets have enormous black markets

that are the only sources for certain basic goods. Here's the point: markets can never be completely denied from a society. The black market is always there to provide customers what they really want. They are the backbone of commerce in any socialist economy.

iii. Finally, socialist countries consistently evidence poor living conditions compared to free market countries. One need only visit a socialist country then a free market country to see the differences. The keynote of socialism is always widespread poverty. This is the curse for denying the truth about God and economics.

C. But there is also a Satanic side to socialism. Denying that sin exists just means it will be more prevalent and unchecked.

i. If a free market ultimately moves toward decentralization of power in countless individuals determining their own lives, socialism moves toward centralization of power into one individual who determines the economic lives of all around him.

ii. By denying God and sin, that person will necessarily be a devil. Some of the great revolutionary socialist leaders are Lenin, Stalin, Hitler, Mao, Pol Pot, and Castro.

iii. In order to control the economic and political actions of a people, it's necessary to have an enormous internal police force to control, and ultimately persecute, its own people.

a. Establishment of a Police State

1) The size of a socialist police force is always many times the size of a police force in a free and Christian nation. This is necessary to ensure that the economic policies of the central planners are carried out.
2) Think about it: socialist governments have to force others to their economic will in terms of managing the factors of production. It's a perfect example of external controls vs. internal controls. And those that violate the political or economic system? They must be physically removed, either by putting them in a labor camp or by executing them.

b. Establishment of a Labor Camp System
   1) The great Christian Russian writer Alexander Solzhenitsyn documented the enormous Russian prison system that enslaved millions of people in his massive work *The Gulag Archipelago*. The title is telling: there was a long island chain of prisons stretching throughout the nation.
   2) In a socialist country, the prisons are for citizens whose crimes may be as insignificant as wanting to work their own way economically, desiring political freedom, or trying to worship God.
   3) Stalin alone put 14 million Russian people in labor camps from 1939–1953—and millions more were imprisoned before and after him.

4) Many other millions have been or still are imprisoned in China, North Korea and Cuba. During the history of the labor camps, many millions died within them. From an economic perspective, this is the enslaving of countless people for their labor with the added benefit of removing them from society.

c. Establishment of Execution Squads

1) For the true enemies of the state—such as many Christians—execution is the best policy. The State sees these people as intractable and necessary to remove permanently from society.

2) As a result, their children are taken away, then they are shot by the police without trial and without recourse to justice. Many tens of millions of men and women have been executed by the police in Russia, China, Cambodia, Vietnam and other socialist countries for their religious beliefs, political beliefs, or because someone in the State simply decreed it.

D. Sin has no check in revolutionary socialism and so it destroys the lives of the people living in that economy.

i. In their attempt to deny God and sin, God gives a socialist economy over to their depravity. As a result, their whole society is consumed in poverty and destruction.

ii. Death is the destiny of the socialist system. And since Christianity is a light that reveals their judgment, it is necessary for the government to remove all traces of it from their society. Wherever socialism reigns, it inevitably wars against Christianity.

4. The Frog in the Pot: *Interventionism & Gradual Socialism* in Practice
   A. This is the current situation we find in the United States as well as in many other countries in the modern world: they fall along the spectrum of interventionist economies.
      i. Unlike revolutionary socialism, which makes radical and swift changes, gradual socialism takes generations to slowly strangle a nation. Like the frog in the slowly heating pot, the cooking may not be noticed until it is too late.
      ii. It has not always been this way. Our founding fathers took sin seriously, and applied those beliefs to our government. They believed that:
         a. Man must be protected from other men. As a result, they passed laws to protect man's freedom, individual rights, and private property.
         b. Man must be protected from the government. So they passed laws to limit the role and reach of government. They believed it was important for men to be stewards with what God had given them.
         c. Before the 1930's, there wasn't a widespread belief that it was the government's responsibility to ensure someone's material well-being. These are not rights in the Biblical or in a Constitutional sense. If the government tries

to offer them, it cannot consistently do so, and will end up bankrupting a nation.

iii. Although our constitutional structure has been broken down in many places by expanding government power and decreasing individual liberty, enough of it remains in place to maintain many freedoms to keep us from immediately falling into the poverty of socialism. But the growth of government services and expectations coupled with recent recessions shows we are slouching toward economic mediocrity.

B. There's not just one contributor to this mediocrity, but countless small ones. The Chinese talk of 'death by 1000 cuts'; that's what we have in the form of our all-powerful *regulatory environment*.

i. Regulation seeks to put external controls on people and industry via endless rules and laws. It is a weaker form of central planning, so it takes longer to hurt a nation.

ii. These external controls are production controls, price controls, hiring controls, labor controls (including minimum and sometimes maximum wages), reporting requirements, and on and on through a labyrinth of regulations that must be followed or the governmental sword will be at one's throat.

iii. To implement all these endless regulations, the government has set up a vast network of government agencies whose names are generally familiar: ICC, FCC, FDA, EPA, OSHA, DHS, HUD, TSA, and literally hundreds more.

iv. The result of all this is that the government depresses individual ability to produce and work by limiting production and even driving companies out of business

C. The important questions are these: 'who stands to gain by this regulation and who stands to lose?' This perspective reveals who is trying to control whom. For instance:

i. Public education tries to control and benefit over private, parental education.

ii. Big business tries to control and benefit over small business.

iii. Unions try to control and benefit over big business.

iv. Special interests try to control and benefit over businesses and individuals.

v. And the list goes on and on. As we all know, someone is always trying to use the government to control someone else. Regulations are a key means of doing so.

D. Some common myths about government regulation that need dispelling:

i. It's said these regulations are "in the public interest."

a. This is code for "someone's interest is being put above someone else's interest." So when you hear those words you need to start wondering who is being taken advantage of to help out someone else?

ii. Wouldn't it be dangerous to remove many of these regulations?

a. Markets created by people are designed to regulate themselves. In other words, businesses and individuals ultimately don't need a government to regulate the details of their lives and work, outside of protecting their liberty and property. They can vote with their pocketbook—and do.

b. There are many non-governmental organizations and industries that have to answer directly to consumers already, and do a great job of it. Take for example Underwriters Laboratories: everyone has seen their famous UL stamped on electrical tools, equipment, and other products. It is an independent company that has been developing standards for product safety since 1894. There are many other companies like this; they do an excellent job self-regulating their industries.

iii. What about people who are dishonest?

a. Punishing dishonesty is actually the purpose of well-written laws that protect private property, not highly targeted regulations created to influence a particular outcome.

b. What we see instead are regulations crafted by some to control others in order to profit from them. *This* is actually dishonest. The difference between good laws and harmful regulations is an important difference; gradual socialism loves lots of little controls over all aspects of an economy.

E. The result of all these regulations is that honest men and women bear the heaviest regulatory burdens.

i. They have to do more paperwork, follow more

rules, hire more lawyers and accountants, add more procedures, and so forth, just to be allowed to operate. These regulatory burdens drive people out of business annually. There is no end in sight—regulations and paperwork follow the same logic of interventionism: more and more are necessary to try to accomplish that ever-elusive objective.

ii. A government-controlled, if not government-owned, regulatory environment means that the government functionally controls many individuals and private businesses without visibly owning and running them.

   a. It tells them what they can and cannot do, then takes a large amount of what they produce. This is a disguised form of socialism, but socialism nonetheless.

   b. It's actually similar to the national socialist programs of Germany and Italy where the government told businesses what they must do, but did not own the businesses outright.

   c. There is another word for it that regularly gets misused in political circles, but when it comes to a nationally controlled economy, is exactly right: *fascism*. You think that's extreme? Try not following some of the regulations and see who shows up.

F. How does sin affect a nation infected with interventionism?

   i. Neither the political system nor the economy has been set up for true central planning and absolute control. However, government intervention in more and more areas of the economy establishes the precedent that government can and should plan and control.

a. As a result, each person or group tries selfishly to manipulate the government to work for his particular economic goals over and against other people's economic goals.

b. Man's sinfulness expresses itself in trying to influence or control some aspect of the government to provide his personal situation either with money or special provisions. This is done in competition with other individuals or groups for the same pot of money and resources.

ii. It results in people viewing the government as a sort of slot machine whose handle has to be pulled in the right way to get what you want.

a. On a personal level, many believe the government is responsible to provide individuals with food, a house, a job, healthcare, and so on. They believe such governmental care "is my right as an American."

b. On a business level, companies want the government to provide more bailouts, subsidies, favorable regulations, special breaks, loans, and any number of other business-enhancing policies.

iii. Some individuals or groups are much better than others at manipulating the government to get what they want.

a. Because our system was set up to be a representative government, most have realized that politicians are the ones who are in the best position to influence outcomes, so they desperately try to control or influence politicians in all sorts of ways, particularly with money.
b. This is the explanation of our current political system where every special interest battles against every other special interest either to get a bigger share of the dwindling government pie, or to get laws passed to better their particular situation in some regulatory fashion.

iv. The situation is sinful in significant ways:
a. People start looking to the government to provide for those in need as opposed to help coming from individuals, community, or church. In this entitlement mindset, the government takes the place of God as provider.
b. There is a loss of personal liberty both economically and politically in slow but steady ways. One need only look back 100 years to see what has been lost. This ensures that Biblical stewardship is curtailed and reduced to minimal impact.
c. It creates an economic system where some are trying to control others through the means of government.
   1) This is a half-way house toward more overt socialism. Instead of there being a

single dictator with a central structure, it's a constant struggle between those who want to take control of the government to use it for their purposes in controlling the market.

2) This results in a slow strangulation of an economy as people look more and more to the government to provide for them and less and less to their own abilities to produce.

v. Over time, a growing anti-Christian sentiment will occur that will seek to use government regulation to control Christianity.

a. Already, we are limited as to where we can talk about Christianity (it's out of schools and anything governmental).

b. We are limited as to how Christians can run their own businesses according to their own views, especially in hiring and healthcare.

c. We are subject to government penalties and threats to try to control pastors and what they talk about.

d. The money and resources produced by Christians are used by the government for ends they morally or economically disagree with: Welfare, Health Services (like contraception), Planned Parenthood (abortion services), Public Education, etc.

e. This movement over generations is a slow tightening of the noose around the necks of Christians. One need only look back 50 years, then 100 years to see the loss in the freedoms of Christians and the diminished place of Christianity in our nation. Much is a result of government action.

vi. Government intervention moves toward socialism gradually through the small but ongoing incursions into individual liberty and business freedom. This transfer of control from individuals to the government affects Christians since the government will seek to circumscribe all actions in accordance with the wills of those individuals who happen to be in control of the government at that time.

5. Free Markets : What about Poverty and Greed?
   A. Throughout this series, we have endeavored to explain how free markets work, arguing that God created men to trade freely with one another in markets under His law.
   B. But how does sin affect free markets? One way is that there's always the sinful tendency of men to try to intervene and manipulate the economy; but we just looked at the consequences of that, and in many ways it's a different economic problem.
   C. Historically, however, there are two complaints lodged against the free market that ultimately are traced back to the effect of sin on men as they seek to work within this (or any) economic system.
      i. The first argument says that the free market increases conditions of poverty within a country, with the rich becoming richer and the poor becoming poorer.

ii. The second argument says that the free market is corrupting morally and encourages greediness and selfishness since it ends up having so much to do with money, trade, and wealth.
iii. Both of these criticisms have been used by socialists for years as arguments against the free market.
   a. But history shows us that socialism will make the poor poorer (as well as the rich poorer) faster than anything else will. Furthermore, the corruption of revolutionary socialist governments leads not only to stealing property, but to labor camps and mass executions!
   b. The corruption of gradual socialist economies leads to the redistribution of huge parts of a nation's wealth either by those in league with the government or by the government itself. This would naturally lead to the rich getting richer and the poor getting poorer.
   c. But there are even simpler answers:

D. The first argument says that free markets make the poor poorer.
   i. There is actually an easy way to answer this question: historical facts consistently show it to be wrong.
   ii. The history of most nations before the eighteenth century was one of poverty. As many economists have noted, the question is not why are some nations poor; rather, the real question is why are any nations wealthy?

a. In the West for the past 250 years, economic trends have only gone in a positive direction: increase in standard of living, increase in life expectancy, increase in healthcare quality, decrease in child mortality, decrease in sickness, decrease in poverty. The facts are indisputable; everyone who lives in the West (and has traveled outside of it) knows it's true.
b. More importantly, during those same years those nations in the West saw a steep increase in missionary activity around the world. Great prosperity was certainly enjoyed by those in the West, but millions of Christians used their surplus money to build up the Kingdom of God as well as to help out the poor around the world.
c. For all the complaints the world lodges against the United States, throughout the twentieth and twenty-first centuries, it has provided more food, disaster, and poverty relief than any other nation in the world. Could it give more? Absolutely. But that's no argument against the free market.

E. Second, does the free market encourage greediness and selfishness?
   i. This has nothing to do with the free market: all people have a tendency to greediness and selfishness, no matter what economy they live in.
   ii. This does not excuse the behavior; but to say that the misuse of prosperity is a problem with an economic system is misplaced blame. In a

free market, people are free to be greedy, just as they are free to be charitable. Their way of acting isn't a result of the system; it's a result of their own internal moral compass.

F. Nevertheless, an interesting study was done in 2010 called *The World Giving Index* that compared the amount of charitable giving and action in the world amongst 153 nations. The results were very interesting.
   i. Here were the countries at the top:
      a. Australia/New Zealand (1)
      b. Canada/Ireland (3)
      c. United States/Switzerland (5)
      d. Netherlands (7)
      e. United Kingdom (8)
   ii. And at the bottom:
      a. Vietnam/Russian Federation (138)
      b. Bulgaria (141)
      c. Cambodia/Romania (142)
      d. China (147)
   iii. Although there were other countries near the bottom, it is telling that the historically Christian and free market countries were first and the historically atheist and socialist countries were last.

6. Closing
   A. Unless an economic system takes sin seriously, it will inevitably be dominated by sin. The more Christian a political system is, the more the effects of sin will be attenuated and minimized across the entire system. This isn't to say that sin is unimportant and without effect: it is not. But on the spectrum of problems that

range from selfishness to stealing to imprisonment to murder, one can see the stark differences between the different economies.

B. As we bring our study to a close, we see that there are dire consequences to economic decisions, consequences that have great bearing upon pursuing stewardship as a Christian in the world.

MULTIPLE CHOICE

1. Proponents of socialism believe that all they need is education, leadership and organization to create a ________ here on earth.
   a. powerful state
   b. utopia
   c. revolution
   d. battlefield

2. Economic calculation is impossible in a socialist economy. ________ will inevitably misallocate a nation's land, labor, and capital because they deny the role of the individual consumer and importance of the market, especially its freedom.
   a. Central planners
   b. Leaders
   c. The populace
   d. Businessmen

3. ________ are consistently seen in socialist communist countries.
   a. Extensive police forces
   b. Prison camps
   c. Execution squads
   d. All of the above

4. _______ seeks to put external controls on people and industry via endless rules and laws.
   a. The free market
   b. Socialism
   c. Regulation
   d. Inflation
5. Government intervention moves toward socialism gradually through the small but ongoing incursions into _______.
   a. individual liberty and business freedom
   b. corporate earnings and individual assets
   c. educational policy
   d. monetary policy

SHORT ANSWER

1. Why do socialist countries consistently seek to persecute Christians?
2. How does a regulatory environment eventually strangle economic growth?
3. Why do you think the complaints of greed and selfishness are primarily used against the free market economy and not interventionist or socialist economies?

DISCUSSION

1. How is stewardship constrained in your lives in terms of the economic situation you find yourself in?
2. Deuteronomy 28 provides economic consequences for moral disobedience to God. Do you think this still bears itself out in modern economic situations?
3. Where do you see economic controls matching up with moral controls in our current society? Should this matter to Christians?

FOR FURTHER STUDY

Unmasking the Sacred Lies—Cleveland—Chapters 4–5, 7, 9–11
Basic Economics, 3rd Ed.—Carson & Cleveland—Chapter 21
Money, Greed and God—Richards—Chapters 4 & 5

Multiple choice answers: 1.b 2.a 3.d 4.c 5.a

12

Kingdom Economics

MESSAGE INTRODUCTION

The cosmic struggle between the seed of the woman and the seed of the serpent has an economic dimension. In this lesson, we'll look at the implications of this struggle on economics and history; at the strategies Christians can use to overcome interventionism; and at the way God is growing His Kingdom in the world.

SCRIPTURE READING

Genesis 3

LEARNING OBJECTIVES

1. To understand the conflict that is going on in history.
2. To see the way Christians can work politically, locally, and in their families.
3. To recognize that God is expanding His Kingdom around the world.

QUOTATIONS

I will put enmity between you and the woman, and between your offspring and her offspring; he shall bruise your head, and you shall bruise his heel (Gen. 3:15).

LECTURE OUTLINE

1. There is a great struggle between the seed of the woman and the seed of the serpent.
   A. Genesis 3:15 marks the beginning of the battle we've been talking about through this entire series. There is a struggle in the world for dominion between the reign of Christ and the reign of Satan.
   B. That dominion has significant economic ramifications with far-reaching issues of control.
      i. We see it in the Bible when the children of Abraham are in Egypt. God prospers them so much that Pharaoh becomes frightened and enslaves them. In other words, they shift suddenly from freedom to a command and control economy where their labor is completely exploited.
      ii. But God sends Moses as His redeemer and the children of Israel are given freedom again. His promise to them also has significant economic ramifications: He will give them His law and take them to a land of milk and honey where they can build a civilization to worship Him.
      iii. From that point forward, the history of Israel fluctuates between freedom and slavery. Their times of greatest economic prosperity come alongside their greatest freedom under David and Solomon; their times of greatest poverty come alongside their bondage to the King of Babylon. With obedience comes prosperity; disobedience brings judgment.
   C. This struggle continues into the Christian era when Alaric sacked Rome in 410 A.D. In light of that con-

quest, St. Augustine wrote *The City of God* to explain how our lives are ultimately lived amidst a battle between Christianity and Atheism.

D. This continues into modern history when in the twentieth century Hitler rose up to try to take over the world. He explained in *Mein Kampf* that he planned to take over Germany, then Europe, then Russia, then Britain, and eventually the United States. Can you image what a hell on earth it would have been had Hitler accomplished his real goals? Is it not obvious that there were dark spiritual powers behind him that sought the domination of the free peoples and the destruction of the Jews?

E. Those who desire to control the lives of other people have not disappeared from the planet. We need to learn our lessons from history or be doomed to repeat them. These issues keep coming up and they exist in our own day. There are people who want to enslave free people all across the globe.

2. How do we push back against the interventionism that leads gradually to socialism?

A. To begin with, Christians need to look at their own sins. What are the ways that we are using government intervention for our own purposes? Are we fighting for the levers of power so we can reach into our neighbors' pockets?

B. We will never have liberty nor will we escape the noose of gradual socialism until we fight against interventionism on behalf of freedom. We have been raised in a context of interventionism, so it shouldn't be surprising if it has greatly affected our thinking.

C. To be faithful soldiers, we need to go into our own minds and hearts and look for those places that the serpent has planted that flag in us. Many of us have been highly influenced by secular education. We should expect that to influence how we think, and we need to correct it with the teaching of the scriptures.
D. Of course, what really needs to motivate us is the desire to help those who have been most profoundly hurt by interventionism. There are real people who are having real hardships because of economic intervention. This is also part of the war between the seed of the woman and the seed of the serpent. We need to come to the rescue of those who are most wounded in this battle.

3. The government we have is the government we voted in. But we can change both it and us. How do we do that?
   A. Christians need to be involved in the political process.
      i. Many Christians today are frustrated by what they see happening around them and just want to give up. That's exactly what Satan wants to have happen.
      ii. Instead, we need to be speaking into the political issues of the day, principally for the sake of those who are being most badly damaged by the bad decisions, the increasing interventionism, and the creeping socialism of our own economic system in America.
      iii. We need not look at the culture around us indifferently, as if it's something outside of our purview as faithful Christians. It's a part of the battle. And we need to speak into those issues. How do we do that?

B. Christians need to speak into issues locally.
   i. We often like to focus on big, national issues, but the reality is that it's at the city, county, metro, and state levels that most of the day-to-day governmental decisions are decided.
   ii. We need to work together to influence the decision makers in our neighborhoods, in our counties, in our states. We can do this with faithful, biblical, sound involvement in the political issues that our local communities are dealing with.
C. Christians need to exercise dominion in their families.
   i. We need to be training our children to understand what is going on around them, the importance of ministries of mercy, of acting politically, of thinking economically. We must teach our children to be involved locally.
   ii. Our individual work and vocations are also the way we exercise dominion. We should seek out ways that we can do our work unto the Lord, working faithfully and diligently at the ways the Lord has called us to serve Him.

4. As we look around the world, we see that God is growing His Kingdom across many nations.
   A. Christianity is on the rise in the East and in the South, with millions of men and women bending their knees to Christ in places that were devoid of the gospel just 100 years ago.
   B. Many of these nations are now Christian as a result of the missionaries that were sent from free countries to evangelize them. Many of these evangelized countries

are beginning to embrace free markets themselves, and some are even sending missionaries back to the free countries that are starting to reject Christianity and the free markets that brought them so much prosperity.

C. Even China, once a picture of Communist control, has started to crumble in places as Christianity and free markets sweep the nation. There is still persecution in this nation, it is still officially communist with a police state and prisons and great antipathy to the gospel. Many things are far from good, but there are literally millions of Christians in what was once the most populous Communist Socialist country in the world. Few people in 1960 would have looked at China under Mao and said that within a hundred years it would be home to the greatest population of Christians in the world. But it will.

5. We have arrived at the end of our study. But let it be just the beginning of yours.
   A. In many ways this series is an introduction to a rich world of economic thinking. There are wonderful books, websites, and seminars from godly men who have spent their careers thinking through these issues. Look at the List of Additional Resources at the front of this study guide for specific recommendations.
   B. Don't stop studying. It is our knowledge and understanding of these things that are a vital part of our weaponry in the battle between the seed of the woman and the seed of the serpent. Satan has worked to keep the church in ignorance of economics for a long time. Use your new knowledge to teach other

Christians the importance of economics to the growth of the Church.

C. Finally, never lose sight of this: the battle is real between the seed of the woman and the seed of the serpent, but we are called to always be of good cheer because Jesus has already overcome the world. *"I have said these things to you, that in me you may have peace. In the world you will have tribulation. But take heart; I have overcome the world"* (John 16:33).

MULTIPLE CHOICE

1. St. Augustine wrote ______ to explain how our lives are ultimately lived amidst a battle between Christianity and Atheism.
   a. On Christian Doctrine
   b. The Confessions
   c. The Immortality of the Soul
   d. The City of God

2. What is the way Christians can push back interventionism?
   a. Be involved in the political process.
   b. Speak into local issues.
   c. Exercise dominion in our families.
   d. All of the above.

3. ______ is a prime example of a communist country that is being converted to Christianity and is also embracing free markets.
   a. Cuba
   b. North Korea
   c. China
   d. Vietnam

SHORT ANSWER

1. What are some contemporary examples of the struggle between the Kingdom of God and the kingdom of Satan in an economic context?

2. How has interventionism affected the thinking of Christians when it comes to the role of the government?

3. What are some specific things you can do to learn more about economics and stewardship?

DISCUSSION

1. What do you think is the most important thing you learned from this series? Why is it important?
2. Studies comparing Christians in the West with Christians in other parts of the world reveal that we think less than others about the battle between Christ and Satan for dominion of the world. Why is this? What does it say about our culture as Christians?
3. If economics is ultimately about being a good steward and expanding God's Kingdom, what can you personally be doing to accomplish this? How can you pursue economics in your own life to the glory of God?

Multiple choice answers: 1.d 2.d 3.c